At My Table

Chelsea Winter

MASTERCHEF NZ WINNER

At My Table

RANDOM HOUSE
NEW ZEALAND

A RANDOM HOUSE BOOK published by
Random House New Zealand
18 Poland Road, Glenfield, Auckland, New Zealand

For more information about our titles go to
www.randomhouse.co.nz

A catalogue record for this book is available from the
National Library of New Zealand

Random House New Zealand is part of the
Random House Group
New York London Sydney Auckland Delhi
Johannesburg

Special thanks to Neat Meat for supplying meat
for the photoshoots

Published 2013, reprinted 2013, 2014 (seven times).

ISBN 978 1 77553 315 3

Design: Kate Barraclough
Photography: Kieran Scott
Styling: Tamara West

Printed in Asia by Leo Paper Products Ltd

Preface

Hi there

Firstly, I'm so glad you've got yourself a copy of my book. I think you're really going to enjoy it! I've filled *At My Table* with my favourite recipes, most of which have fond memories attached to them. Many of them I've cooked countless times for family and friends over the years; some have been passed down through the generations. It's totally inspiring to know that lovely people like you are serving them up in every corner of New Zealand (and beyond!).

I also just have to say, what's so fantastic is the feedback I receive every day about this book. Countless people take the time out of their busy lives to thank me for the recipes they love. It means the world to me, and I hope you feel the same way after you've given them a good go yourself. If you'd ever like to get in touch, or if you have any questions, you can always get hold of me via my Facebook page (www.facebook.com/ChelseaWinterDelicious) or website (www.chelseawinter.co.nz). I'd love to hear from you.

Right – I'll leave you to browse and pick a recipe to make first. I hope you enjoy using my cookbook as much as I enjoyed creating it! May it take you on a jaunty lifelong journey of utter deliciousness.

My parting words to you are: don't be scared of a little pure butter. It makes the world a far better place.

I wish you the warmest regards and loads of happy cooking,

Chels xx

Chapter one

Breakfast

Serves 2–3

Smoky baked beans

Yes, it's baked beans, but not as you know them . . . so if you're not currently a baked beans fan, don't turn the page over in horror just yet! If you're looking for something a little different for your next lazy weekend brunch, then why not serve up these fresh homemade baked beans piled on hot buttered toast? The textures and flavours are a far cry from the sweet, over-salted blob of beans you dig out of a can. If tomatoes are in season, chop up a couple of ripe ones and add them in for a hit of summer freshness. For the hungriest customers, serve the beans with a couple of poached eggs, some crispy bacon, a steaming hot coffee and *voilà* – you've got a breakfast worthy of any café in town.

1 tbsp olive oil
1 onion, finely chopped
1 clove garlic, chopped
2 x 400g cans chopped tomatoes
2 x 420g cans butter or cannellini beans
1 tsp paprika
½ tsp smoked paprika
2 tsp chopped fresh oregano leaves
1 bay leaf
½ tsp mustard powder
1 cup chicken or vegetable stock
few drops Worcestershire sauce
3 tsp sugar
2 tsp malt or white wine vinegar
salt and freshly cracked black pepper
buttered toast to serve
freshly grated parmesan to serve
chopped fresh parsley leaves to serve

Heat the olive oil in a large frying pan over a medium heat. Add the onion and garlic, and cook for 5 minutes until soft. Add the tomatoes, beans, paprikas, oregano, bay leaf, mustard powder and stock, and stir to combine. Simmer gently for 15 minutes or until the sauce has reduced and thickened enough. Stir in the Worcestershire sauce, sugar and vinegar, then taste and season with salt and pepper.

Serve on buttered toast and garnish with the parmesan and parsley. Add some poached eggs (see page 16) if you like.

Serves 3–4

Chorizo and mushrooms on toast

This is the ultimate weekend brunch treat, and it's a dish I love making because everyone goes so crazy for it. While everyone is snoring away in the morning, I'll potter around in the kitchen cooking this. The gorgeous aromas snake around the house, and soon enough people are up and making a beeline for the kitchen! The combination of the creamy garlicky mushrooms and lightly spiced chorizo is hard to beat. If you don't have chorizo, you can serve it with crispy bacon instead.

2 tsp olive oil
150g chorizo sausages, sliced
25g butter
4 cloves garlic, finely chopped
400g button mushrooms, chopped
1–2 portobello mushrooms, chopped
½ cup dry white wine
¾ cup cream
½ tsp cornflour mixed with a little water
½ tsp vegetable stock powder
2 cups baby spinach leaves
salt and freshly cracked black pepper
4 free-range eggs, poached (see page 16)
4–6 slices toast (I use ciabatta)
torn fresh basil leaves to garnish
grated fresh parmesan to garnish

Heat the olive oil in a frying pan over a high heat. Fry the chorizo slices for 4–5 minutes, stirring until coloured. Remove and drain on paper towels.

Turn the heat down to medium and add the butter to the pan. Add the garlic and sauté for 3 minutes. Add the two kinds of mushrooms and stir for a few minutes. Turn the heat up to high, add the white wine and let it bubble for 30 seconds. Reduce the heat to medium-high and reduce the wine by two-thirds, about 5 minutes. Add the cream, cornflour mix, stock powder, fried chorizo and spinach leaves, and simmer for 7–10 minutes until the sauce has thickened and the mushrooms are cooked. Taste and season with salt and pepper.

Poach the eggs following the method on page 16 while the mushrooms are cooking, and rest on paper towels.

Spoon the mushrooms onto buttered toast, top with a poached egg, sprinkle with the chopped basil and the parmesan, and season with salt and pepper.

Serves 3–4

French lace pancakes

I've been making these pancakes since I was just a wee thing needing a stool to reach the benchtop. I'd make a colossal mess, eat half the raw batter and burn myself turning the frying pan but, boy, did I love it. To me, these are pancakes as they should be. Light and thin with beautiful buttery, crispy lace-like patterns. Those thick, stodgy American pancakes can leave you feeling like you've got a great lump of dough sitting in your stomach, but these ones are delicate and beautiful. To serve, I think all they need is a little lemon juice and a dusting of icing sugar. But you can go as wild as you like – the fridge's the limit.

1½ cups plain flour
pinch salt
1 free-range egg
2 cups milk
25g butter, melted
butter for cooking

Sift the flour and salt into a large mixing bowl. Make a well in the centre and add the egg and milk. Whisk gently in the middle, slowly incorporating the flour from the outside until the batter is smooth and well mixed. Add the melted butter and whisk to just combine. Cover and rest for 30 minutes.

Preheat the oven to 50°C.

Heat a medium-sized frying pan over a medium heat. Add 1 teaspoon of butter and swirl to coat the bottom of the pan. Add a ladleful of the pancake batter and swirl the pan so you get a nice circular pancake. Cook for a couple of minutes, until golden brown, then flip over using a fish slice. Cook for another couple of minutes until golden on the other side. Place on a plate in the oven while you cook the rest, adding more butter to the pan when needed.

Serve the pancakes with whatever takes your fancy: fresh lemon juice and icing sugar, maple syrup, fruit and cream, or bacon, walnut and banana. Or a bit of everything!

Serves 2

Eggs Benedict

Good old eggs Bene is perhaps the most quintessential Kiwi café breakfast there is. Visually impressive, decadent and often avoided by the home cook because of the scary hollandaise. Which is silly, as it's so easy to make once you know how. Homemade breakfasts like this are fantastic, because after you've gone to a café and had a couple of coffees, juices and two breakfasts, you'll often find there's a massive smoking hole in your wallet where your cash used to be. Sometimes it's nicer to avoid the crowds, chilling out at home with your own fancy breakfast and some good music. It's a great way to start the day in my books! For a vege option, pop a nice grilled portobello mushroom and some sautéed spinach on the toast instead.

4 free-range eggs
small pinch salt
¼ cup white vinegar
1 free-range egg yolk
1 tsp lemon juice
¼ tsp cayenne pepper
50g butter, melted
4 slices toast (I use ciabatta) to serve
4 slices cooked crispy bacon or smoked salmon to serve
salt and freshly cracked black pepper
fresh parsley and dill leaves to garnish

Gently crack the eggs into a bowl and set aside.

Half fill a large saucepan with water. Season with the salt and add the vinegar. Cover and bring to a gentle rolling boil.

Bring another smaller saucepan of water to a very gentle simmer. Do not boil.

In a small heatproof bowl, whisk the egg yolk with the lemon juice until light and creamy. Add the cayenne pepper and a small pinch of salt. Place the bowl with the egg yolk mixture over the simmering water and slowly add the melted butter, whisking continuously. Continue to whisk the sauce for about 5 minutes until it thickens. Be very careful not to overcook or overheat the egg, as it will scramble and split. Set aside while you poach the eggs.

Swirl the boiling water in the large pan around in a circle to create a gentle whirlpool. Carefully tip the eggs into the centre. Reduce to a simmer and cook for 3 minutes, more if you don't like runny eggs. Gently lift the eggs out with a slotted spoon and drain on paper towels.

Butter the toast, top with the cooked bacon or smoked salmon, then the poached eggs. If the hollandaise sauce has got a little thick, add 1 teaspoon of boiling water and whisk again. Pour the sauce over the eggs. Season with salt and pepper, and garnish with the herbs.

Serves 3–4

French toast

I love starting the day on a sweet note sometimes, and this classic is another dish I've been making since I was just a tyke. If you haven't tried the combination of crunchy bacon and caramelised banana yet, you're missing out on a very good thing. Salty, sweet, syrupy and creamy with a nice crunch of walnut. If you don't have walnuts, you could try macadamias or chopped almonds. A squeeze of lemon can also be a nice touch for a little cut-through. If you were feeling very decadent, I would recommend adding a little scoop of ice-cream to the plate. Slightly hedonistic? Yes, but I won't tell if you won't.

4 free-range eggs
½ cup milk
¼ cup cream
zest of 1 lemon
½ tsp ground cinnamon
few drops vanilla essence
2–3 bananas, skin on, halved lengthways
2 tbsp sugar
3 tbsp butter
½ cup chopped walnuts
1 loaf day-old ciabatta, cut into 2–3cm thick slices
4–6 rashers cooked crispy bacon
maple syrup to serve
lemon wedges to serve

Preheat the oven to 50°C.

Put the eggs, milk, cream, lemon zest, cinnamon and vanilla in a bowl. Whisk together very well until the egg is fully incorporated into the mixture. Set aside.

Sprinkle the flesh of the bananas with the sugar.

Heat 2 tablespoons of butter in a frying pan over a medium heat and add the bananas cut side down. Sprinkle the walnuts around the edges and in the gaps so they caramelise a little too. Cook for 5 minutes or until the bananas are golden brown but not quite cooked through.

Heat 1 tablespoon of butter in another frying pan over a medium-high heat. Dip the bread slices into the egg mixture until soaked through, then add to the pan. Fry for a few minutes on each side until golden and crispy and cooked right through. Keep warm in the oven while you fry the remaining bread.

Serve with the banana and walnuts, along with crispy bacon, maple syrup and lemon wedges.

Chapter two
Baking

Makes about 18

Afghans

Back when I was a little girl at primary school, you could order a tuck-shop lunch once a week. A big bucket filled with little paper bags of pies and goodies would turn up in the classroom. While most kids gobbled jam doughnuts for the sweet treat, I always went for the afghans.

I still love them, and these mini afghans are just delicious. Trying to combine the cornflakes into the mixture can be awkward as it seems like there are far too many, but you just need to use some elbow grease – don't worry if you crunch them up.

225g butter
½ cup sugar
1 tsp vanilla essence
185g plain flour
½ cup cocoa
3 cups cornflakes
⅓ cup desiccated coconut

Icing

1 cup icing sugar, sifted
2 tbsp cocoa
1 tbsp butter, softened
1 tbsp boiling water
walnut halves for decorating

Preheat the oven to 170°C. Line a baking tray with baking paper.

Cream the butter and sugar together for about 5 minutes until pale and thick. Add the vanilla and beat until combined.

Sift in the flour and cocoa, and mix well. Lastly add the cornflakes and coconut, and fold together until combined.

Place tablespoonsful of the mixture onto the lined baking tray, and press down very gently with a fork. Bake in the oven for 11–13 minutes. Cool for 10 minutes on the tray, then transfer to a wire rack.

To make the icing, beat the icing sugar, cocoa, butter and water until well combined. Add a little more water if necessary. Ice the cooled afghans and top with a walnut half.

May be stored in an airtight container for a week.

Makes about 30

Incredibly tasty cookies

These cookies are another childhood favourite of mine. Don't be fooled by their humble and homely exterior; they're crammed with lots of delicious things and absolutely scrumptious to eat. I think the ground oats add a really lovely creamy, wholesome flavour, too. This recipe makes a whole load of cookies, so you can share them around with the troops.

2 cups rolled oats
200g butter
½ cup white sugar
1 cup soft brown sugar
2 free-range eggs
1 tsp vanilla essence
2 cups plain flour
1 tsp baking powder
1 tsp baking soda
½ tsp salt
300g chocolate chips or good-quality chocolate, chopped
1 cup chopped nuts of your choice (almonds, peanuts, pecans, macadamias, walnuts)

Preheat the oven to 180°C. Line a baking tray with baking paper.

Place the rolled oats in a food processor and blend to a powder.

Cream the butter and both sugars together until pale and thick. Add the eggs, one at a time, beating well after each addition, then add the vanilla and beat to combine.

Mix the rolled oats, flour, baking powder, baking soda and salt together. Add to the creamed mixture and mix to combine. Fold in the chocolate chips or chopped chocolate and nuts.

Roll into tablespoon-sized balls and place 5cm apart on the prepared tray (you will probably need to bake them in batches). Bake in the oven for 10–12 minutes. Remove and cool for 5 minutes on the tray, then transfer to a wire rack.

May be stored in an airtight container for 1–2 weeks.

Makes about 12 slices

Nana's caramel slice

I love anything with caramel in it, and this recipe from my nana's archives is definitely one to keep on hand. The biscuit base stays lovely and soft and crumbly. So many of the other slices I've tried have a hard crunchy base, but I much prefer it delicate and buttery like this. Thanks, Nana, lots of love!

Base
220g butter
85g sugar
1 free-range egg, lightly beaten
170g plain flour
½ cup ground almonds
pinch salt

Caramel
85g butter
¾ cup soft brown sugar
2 tbsp golden syrup
½ cup sweetened condensed milk
2 tbsp plain flour

Icing
200g good-quality dark chocolate
50g butter

Preheat the oven to 190°C. Grease and line a 32cm x 22cm slice tin.

Cream the butter and sugar together until thick and pale. (I use a food processor for this and scrape down the sides every now and then.) Beat in the egg until well incorporated, then add the flour, ground almonds and salt. Beat until combined. Pour into the prepared slice tin and spread out in an even layer with a spatula.

Bake in the oven for 18 minutes. Remove the base from the oven.

To make the caramel filling, place all the ingredients in a saucepan and melt over a medium heat, stirring to combine, until the sugar has dissolved. Pour the mixture onto the hot base in an even layer, then return to the oven for another 10 minutes.

Remove the slice from the oven and cool in the tin before icing.

To make the icing, gently melt the chocolate and butter in a heatproof bowl placed over a saucepan of gently simmering water, stirring gently to combine. Pour over the top of the caramel, and place in the fridge for 20 minutes to set.

Cut into slices and serve.

May be stored in an airtight container in the fridge for up to a week.

Makes about 12 slices

Oaty ginger crunch

I have a sweet tooth and I always like to have some nice slice around. I think there's something to be said for having a little bit of sweetness to enjoy with your mid-morning cuppa – it just seems to brighten up the day, especially if you're stressing out behind a desk at work or frazzled at home. It's the simple little pleasures in life that we should remember to take the time out for. Forget the diet for a second, forget the annoying emails, forget the errands and the housework . . . just enjoy.

Base
150g butter
¾ cup soft brown sugar
2 tbsp golden syrup
¾ cup plain flour
1½ tsp baking powder
1½ tsp ground ginger
1½ cups whole oats
¾ cup desiccated coconut

Icing
150g butter
2 cups icing sugar, sifted
3 tbsp golden syrup
4 tsp ground ginger

Preheat the oven to 180°C. Grease a 32cm x 22cm slice tin and line the base with baking paper.

Melt the butter, sugar and golden syrup in a large saucepan over a medium heat, stirring gently to combine. Remove from the heat.

Sift the flour, baking powder and ginger into the pan with the caramel. Add the oats and coconut, and fold to combine. Press the mixture into the prepared tin, and smooth out with the back of a spoon.

Bake in the oven for 15 minutes. Remove and leave in the tin.

Heat the icing ingredients in a saucepan, stirring over a medium heat until melted. Pour over the warm slice. Leave in the tin to cool, then cut into slices.

May be stored in an airtight container in the fridge for up to a week.

Makes about 10 scones

Lemonade and cream scones

I know that, for me, the thought of making scones used to conjure up images of a messy array of butter and flour, only to be rewarded with sad scone rocks at the end. No more! This recipe is genius in its simplicity, and it works. We used to whip these up at Great Barrier in summer for a sugary treat after a day's swimming.

Scones
3 cups self-raising flour
¼ tsp salt
1 cup full cream
1 cup lemonade (not sugar-free)

Quick berry jam
1½ cups frozen mixed berries
½ cup sugar
zest of 1 lemon

whipped cream to serve

Preheat the oven to 220°C. Line a baking tray with baking paper.

Sift the flour and salt into a large mixing bowl and make a well in the centre. Pour the cream and lemonade into the well, then use a butter knife to gently mix in circles until the ingredients just come together to form a wet dough. Don't overmix or stir too vigorously.

Tip the dough out onto a floured benchtop and knead it gently a few times. Shape and pat it into a circle about 2–3cm high. Use a round cookie cutter to cut rounds out of the dough, and place on the prepared tray. Bake in the oven for 12–15 minutes until golden on top.

While the scones are cooking, make the jam. Place all the ingredients in a saucepan over a medium heat and simmer for 10 minutes or until a jam-like consistency.

Remove the scones from the oven and cool a little on a wire rack. If you don't eat them all at once, they'll keep for a day.

For the most pleasurable scone-eating experience, you need to eat them while they are still nice and warm with lots of the berry jam and whipped cream.

Makes about 10 pieces

Triple-chocolate brownie

Who doesn't love a good brownie? They're fabulous not only for the obvious reason, i.e. they're loaded with gorgeous chocolate, but also because they're so quick and easy to whip up. I kicked the chocolate quotient up a notch with this one, as I like the way the chocolate pieces add a chunky bite to the slice. You can either slice the brownie into pieces, or serve it whole on a platter, pile on whipped cream, chocolate sauce and fresh berries and devour it as a dessert.

100g butter
1 cup sugar
2 free-range eggs
1 tsp vanilla essence
¾ cup plain flour
1 tsp baking powder
½ cup cocoa
100g good-quality white chocolate, cut into small chunks
100g good-quality dark chocolate, cut into small chunks
icing sugar to dust (optional)

Preheat the oven to 180°C. Grease a 22cm x 22cm slice tin, and line the base with baking paper.

Melt the butter in a saucepan over a low heat. Remove from the heat, and whisk in the sugar. Add the eggs and vanilla, and whisk to combine. Sift the flour, baking powder and cocoa into the mixture. Add the white and dark chocolate chunks, and very gently fold in with a wooden spoon or spatula until only just combined. Do not overmix or the brownie will toughen. Pour the mixture into the prepared tin.

Bake in the oven for about 20 minutes, then test with a skewer. These brownies are done if the skewer still has a little of the mixture clinging to it. Remove from the oven and cool in the tin before slicing. Dust with icing sugar if you wish.

May be stored in an airtight container for a week.

Makes about 16

Coconut cookies

This cute little recipe is ridiculously quick and easy – a great one for the kids. There's no fussing around; just mix everything up, shape and bake. You'll have a lovely batch of coconut cookies that are chewy on the outside and soft on the inside. Drizzle melted chocolate over the cookies as I've done here to make them extra special if you like, or even sandwich them together with lemon icing.

100g butter
100g sugar
1 free-range egg
2 tbsp plain flour
½ tsp vanilla essence
125g desiccated or shredded coconut
zest of 1 lemon

Preheat the oven to 180°C. Line a baking tray with baking paper.

Cream the butter and sugar together until thick and pale. Add the egg and beat well to combine, then beat in the flour and vanilla. Mix in the coconut and lemon zest.

Drop tablespoon-sized balls onto the prepared tray and bake in the oven for 12–15 minutes or until golden. You may need to turn the baking tray around halfway through if they are not cooking evenly. Cool on a wire rack.

May be stored in an airtight container for a week.

Makes 8 assembled biscuits

Berry melting moments

My mum would buy melting moments as a treat whenever we were at a bakery or café when I was younger and I love the way they really do melt in your mouth. The fresh pop of berry in this recipe is a nice change from the usual lemon, plus it looks great. They can be made in a food processor, which is another very good reason to love them! The recipe makes 8 biscuits when assembled, so if you're catering for a crowd just double the recipe.

Biscuits

130g butter
¼ cup icing sugar
1 tsp vanilla essence
¾ cup plain flour
½ tsp baking powder
⅓ cup cornflour
icing sugar for dusting

Filling

1 cup frozen mixed berries
2 tbsp butter, softened
1 cup icing sugar

Preheat the oven to 160°C. Line a baking tray with baking paper.

Cream the butter and icing sugar together, then add the vanilla. Combine the flour, baking powder and cornflour and beat in to form a slightly crumbly dough.

Roll into walnut-sized balls and place 6cm apart on the prepared tray. Gently press down with a fork dipped in a little cornflour.

Bake in the oven for 10–12 minutes until just starting to colour. Cool completely on the tray, then dust with icing sugar.

To make the filling, heat the berries in a small saucepan over a medium heat, stirring until most of the liquid has evaporated; 5–10 minutes. Cool slightly, then beat together with the butter and icing sugar until well combined. Cool until the mixture thickens, adding more icing sugar if necessary. Then sandwich the melting moments together with the filling.

May be stored in an airtight container for a week.

Makes 1 largish cake

Carrot cake with cream cheese icing

This delicious carrot cake recipe has been in our family for as long as I can remember. Mum always made it in the same big heart-shaped tin that all my birthday cakes were cooked in. I think it's quite appropriate because there's certainly a lot to love about this cake – it's rich, moist, carroty, lightly spiced and the delectable creamy icing finishes it all off to perfection. It's impressive to look at, too – a welcome treat for any special occasion (or even to make just because).

Cake

5 free-range eggs
1¾ cups caster sugar
1½ cups oil (sunflower, rice bran, safflower or canola)
2 cups plain flour
1 cup self-raising flour
2 tsp baking soda
3 tsp ground cinnamon
½ tsp ground ginger
¼ tsp ground cloves
¼ tsp ground nutmeg
pinch salt
¾ cup chopped walnuts (optional)
¾ cup raisins or sultanas
3 cups peeled and grated carrot

Icing

3 cups icing sugar, sifted
75g softened butter
juice and zest of 1 lemon
250g cream cheese

Preheat the oven to 160°C. Grease a 24cm to 26cm cake tin.

Crack the eggs into a large bowl. Add the sugar and whisk gently to dissolve the sugar. Add the oil and mix to combine. Sift in the flours, baking soda, spices and salt, and stir gently. Add the nuts if using, the raisins or sultanas and the grated carrot. Stir with a fork to combine (do not beat). Pour into the prepared tin.

Bake in the oven for about 1½ hours or until a skewer inserted in the centre comes out clean – start checking after 1 hour 10 minutes. Cool slightly in the tin, then turn out onto a wire rack.

To make the icing, beat all the ingredients together with an electric beater until thick and smooth. Add a little more lemon juice if necessary to thin it out, or more icing sugar if it's too thin. Ice the cooled cake using a knife dipped in hot water.

Makes 1 large cake

Mighty chocolate cake with ganache icing

This tastes as good as any cake I've bought from a shop, and it's very hard to get it wrong. I've had some awful experiences with chocolate cakes being dry, not rich enough, not dark enough, all crusty on the outside, or sometimes just too small and disappointing. This is a monster of a cake and although it's just one layer, it stays beautifully moist all the way through. The shiny ganache icing is a simple, elegant way to finish it off and the berries add a pop of colour and freshness. Whether you make this to enjoy with the family or as a gift for some lucky person, I can assure you it will be devoured with gusto!

Cake

2½ cups plain flour
1¼ cups cocoa
3 tsp baking soda
1½ tsp baking powder
1 tsp salt
3 cups caster sugar
3 free-range eggs, lightly beaten
1½ tsp vanilla essence
1½ cups strong coffee, cooled
1½ cups buttermilk (or add 1 tbsp lemon juice to milk and leave for 5–10 minutes)
1 cup oil (rice bran, sunflower or canola)

Icing

400g good-quality dark chocolate, chopped into pieces
400ml cream
50g butter

fresh berries for serving

Preheat the oven to 170°C. Grease and flour a 24cm to 26cm springform cake tin.

Sift all the dry ingredients except the sugar together in the biggest mixing bowl you have and mix well to combine. Make a well in the centre.

Place the sugar and all the wet ingredients in a large bowl and whisk gently for a few minutes until everything is well combined.

Slowly add to the dry mixture, stirring until only just combined. Pour into the prepared tin.

Bake for 1½ hours or until a skewer inserted in the centre comes out clean – start checking after 1 hour. Cool in the tin, then turn out onto a wire rack.

To make the icing, melt the chocolate with the cream and butter in a heatproof bowl over a saucepan of barely simmering water, stirring until melted and well combined. Leave to cool until it just reaches icing consistency – not too runny or firm. You may need to pop it in the fridge. Ice the cooled cake with a hot knife and serve with berries on top.

Makes 1 medium-sized cake

Oma's one and only Dutch apple tart

This wonderfully moist spiced apple tart (which is really more of a cake) reminds me of going to Fieldays back when I was about five. We had a family stall there and sold bacon and egg buns, tea, coffee and warm slices of this homemade apple tart with cream to lots of hungry farmers. The food was such a hit that the queues ran around the block – and the year after, a few knockoff stalls appeared offering the very same menu!

This is an old family recipe and there's something so comforting and homely about it. Have it with a hot drink and a big blob of blueberry cream or ice-cream, and you'll be in seventh heaven.

5–6 medium apples (I use Granny Smith)
1 tbsp lemon zest
1 tbsp lemon juice
1 tbsp ground cinnamon
1 tsp mixed spice
½ tsp ground ginger
1 tbsp sugar
150g butter, softened slightly and cubed
200g sugar
3 free-range eggs
1 tsp vanilla essence
220g plain flour
1 tsp baking powder
3 tbsp milk
½ cup blueberries
2 tbsp apricot jam
1 tbsp boiling water
whipped cream to serve
handful blueberries to serve

Preheat the oven to 160°C fan-bake. Grease a 20cm springform cake tin with butter and dust with a little flour, shaking off the excess.

Peel the apples and quarter into the most even-sized pieces possible. Remove the cores. Cut each quarter into 2–3 even-sized pieces. Place the apple slices in a large bowl and add the lemon zest and juice, cinnamon, mixed spice, ginger and the first measure of sugar. Mix well to combine and coat the apple. Set aside.

Cream the butter and second measure of sugar together until thick and pale – you can use a food processor if you have one. Add the eggs, one at a time, beating after each addition. Then add the vanilla. Add the flour and baking powder and beat until just combined. (Sift them into the mixture if you are beating by hand.) Now beat in the milk. You should have a thick, creamy batter.

Spread a thin layer of batter over the base of the tin. Give the apple another stir, then gently place a ring of apple slices very close together all the way round the inside edge of the tin, lightly pressing them down. Put the 'fat' end of each slice towards the outside of the tin; it helps them fit better. Repeat with another ring inside each previous ring until the whole layer of batter is covered with circles of apple – place a few extra slices in the middle to fill the hole, and fill any big gaps. Pour half of the

Recipe continued over page

lemony liquid in the bottom of the apple bowl over the apples. Scatter the half cup of blueberries over evenly.

Pour all the remaining batter over the top, and spread in an even layer – Oma used a slice of apple to do this; I use a spatula! Add another layer of apple slices in decreasing circles again. Pour any remaining juice from the apple bowl over the top.

Bake in the oven for 1 hour or until golden, puffy and set in the middle.

To make a glaze, mix the apricot jam with the boiling water, and brush it generously over the top of the cake with a pastry brush. Make sure you get into all the gaps!

Serve warm with the whipped cream and blueberries or ice-cream. If you like, you can mash a handful of blueberries into the whipped cream along with a little icing sugar to make blueberry cream.

Store in an airtight container out of the fridge – the flavours intensify a day later. It will keep for about a week.

Serves about 12

Speculaas – Dutch spiced cake with almond filling

With a spiced shortcake on the outside and a delightfully surprising gummy almond centre, this special family cake is a legend in its own right. It reminds me of my oma more than anything else – there was always one in her pantry when we went to visit, and we were never denied a slice (plus one to take home). A Christmas gift of a speculaas was the most coveted of all! Once you've made it for yourself, you'll understand why. This cake keeps for weeks in a tin.

Filling

175g ground almonds
175g sugar
1 large free-range egg
zest of 1 large lemon or 2 small lemons

Cake

175g hard butter
175g soft brown sugar
2 cups self-raising flour
2 tsp ground cinnamon
1 tsp mixed spice
½ tsp ground nutmeg
½ tsp ground cloves
2–3 tbsp milk
cream for brushing
blanched peeled almonds to decorate

To make the filling, place all the ingredients in a bowl and mix together well. Shape into a ball and wrap in cling film. Leave in the fridge for as long as possible – overnight if you're rushed; a week or even a month for best results. I usually make a double batch for this reason!

Preheat the oven to 170°C. Grease a 22cm to 23cm round springform cake tin.

Process the butter and sugar together in a food processor for a few minutes until well combined. Add the flour and spices and process again. With the motor running, slowly add just enough milk for the mixture to form a doughy ball.

Spread half the mixture into the prepared tin, and with clean, moistened fingers press down to spread it out smoothly and evenly. Roll out the cold almond mixture between two pieces of baking paper into a disc about the same size as the tin, then place on top of the bottom layer of mixture. Use your fingers to press it out to the sides in an even layer. Add the last half of the dough mixture on top, and spread out evenly with moistened fingers. Brush the top with a little cream and arrange the blanched almonds on the top.

Bake in the oven for 40 minutes until golden brown and shiny. Remove and cool for a few minutes in the tin, then turn out onto a wire rack.

Slice and enjoy with a nice cuppa.

Makes 1 loaf

Barrier beer bread

If there was any one food that represented my long childhood summer holidays at Medlands Beach on Great Barrier Island, this much-loved homemade bread would probably be it. The recipe is from our tattered handwritten bach recipe book, and it's been used so many times it's now a smudgy mess! I'm glad that it's in this book so it will be preserved for a few more years yet (and you can enjoy it, too).

3 cups plain flour
3 tsp baking powder
1 tsp salt
2 tsp sugar
375ml bottle beer
topping of your choice: pumpkin or sunflower seeds, parmesan cheese, red onion, pinenuts, sundried tomato, chargrilled capsicum, pesto
1 tbsp extra virgin olive oil

Preheat the oven to 180°C. Grease and flour a loaf tin.

Sift all the dry ingredients together in a large bowl and mix well. Add the beer and fold in gently until just combined. Pour the mixture into the prepared tin. Add your choice of toppings and drizzle with the olive oil.

Bake in the oven for about 40 minutes, or until golden and the loaf sounds hollow when tapped and a skewer inserted in the centre comes out clean.

Enjoy fresh out of the oven with lots of butter, a salad, leftover meat or tuna etc.

Captage d'altitude
L'Enchapleuze
2074 m.

Chapter three

Lunch and small plates

Serves 4

Buffalo chicken nibbles with blue cheese aïoli and spicy dipping sauce

Behold, my ultimate signature dish! Before this book, only two people had the recipe, but I want to share it with you because it's too good to be kept under wraps. I'm not even going to be modest: I think one of my crunchy chicken nibbles dunked in creamy blue cheese sauce is as close to taste perfection as you can get – and my friends and family agree! We've spent many a sunny afternoon on the deck with a cold beer in hand, a giant pile of wings in front of us, great music playing and a game of cards on the go. Now you can do the same. Enjoy!

Aïoli

1 free-range egg
1 clove garlic, roughly chopped
2 tsp lemon juice
1 cup rice bran or canola oil
100g blue cheese, chopped roughly
1–2 tbsp finely chopped fresh parsley leaves
salt and pepper

Hot sauce

100g butter
1 x 60ml bottle Tabasco
1 tsp smoked paprika
1 tsp sugar
1 tsp salt

Nibbles

¾ cup plain flour
2 tsp salt
1–2kg chicken nibbles
rice bran or canola oil for frying

carrot and celery sticks to serve

To make the aïoli, place the egg, garlic and lemon juice in a small food processor and blend until well mixed. With the motor running, slowly add the oil in a thin stream. The mixture will thicken. Add the blue cheese and parsley, and process until well combined. Taste and season with salt and freshly cracked black pepper. Set aside.

To make the sauce, slowly melt the butter in a small saucepan without stirring. Gently pour the yellow liquid into a bowl, leaving the white milk solids behind. Discard the milk solids. Add the whole bottle of Tabasco, paprika, sugar and salt, and whisk to combine. Set aside.

Preheat the oven to 50°C.

Mix the flour and salt in a bowl, then toss the nibbles in the mixture to coat. You may need more flour and salt, depending on how many nibbles you have. Set aside while you heat the oil.

Fill a saucepan with enough oil to half submerge the nibbles and heat to medium-high. Cook the chicken in batches for around 4–5 minutes on each side until golden brown and cooked through. Drain on paper towels, sprinkle with salt and place in the oven to keep warm while you cook the remaining nibbles.

You can either coat the chicken in the hot sauce, or serve it on the side as a dip along with the blue cheese aïoli. Add some carrot and celery sticks to the plate to serve.

Serves 2

Summer chicken salad

In the heat of the summer, a fresh chicken salad is a great light meal to serve. You can be as creative as you like with what ingredients you add – just use what's in season and you can't really go wrong. I like to add asparagus when it's around, for example. I leave the skin on the chicken for flavour and moisture, but leave it off if you like.

Herb and feta dressing

2 tbsp mayonnaise or aïoli (see page 210)
¼ cup feta
2 tbsp lemon juice, or to taste
2 tbsp olive oil
¼ cup finely chopped fresh coriander leaves and stalks
¼ cup finely chopped fresh basil leaves
1 tsp honey

Chicken

olive oil for cooking
2 large boneless chicken breasts
1 tsp paprika

Salad

1–2 cups mixed salad leaves, tossed in a little extra virgin olive oil and lemon
½ red onion, thinly sliced
½ cup ripe cherry tomatoes
1–2 stalks celery, chopped
1 cob cooked sweetcorn, kernels cut off
1 avocado, sliced
¼ cup fresh mint leaves
handful crispy noodles

Preheat the oven to 220°C.

To make the dressing, process all the ingredients in a food processor. Taste and season with salt and freshly cracked black pepper, and add more honey or lemon juice to your liking.

Heat a little olive oil in a frying pan over a high heat. Season the chicken breasts with salt and pepper, and sprinkle the paprika on one side. Cook, skin side down, for a few minutes until golden and crispy. Turn over and cook for another minute or two.

Transfer to a baking dish and bake in the oven for 12–15 minutes depending on the size of the breast. Remove from the oven and rest for 10 minutes, then slice thinly.

Arrange the salad ingredients on a plate, top with the chicken and drizzle the dressing over.

Makes 2–3 ramekins

Chicken liver pâté with pear glaze

I'm a big fan of drinks and nibbles. Give me gorgeous big platters overflowing with cheeses, dips, tangy pickles, salty olives and, of course, pâté – one of my favourite platter staples. I created this recipe one day after I saw a pottle of livers at the supermarket and decided to have a crack at making my own pâté. It was so delightfully easy I've made it many times since, and had some very happy dinner guests as a result. Despite what I've said above, you don't really need a platterful of things to enjoy this pâté – I sometimes just spread it thickly on slices of crunchy Vogel's toast, and it's divine.

350g chicken livers
1 tbsp butter
1 shallot, chopped
1 clove garlic, chopped
2 tsp chopped fresh thyme or sage leaves (or a mixture of both)
¼ cup brandy
50g butter, cubed
¼ cup cream
salt and freshly cracked black pepper
1 x 100g container pear paste
2 tbsp medium white wine

Grease 2–3 ramekins or 1 large bowl.

Trim the chicken livers to remove all the fat, looking out for any greenish patches – cut these off as they will make the pâté bitter.

Heat the first measure of butter in a frying pan over a medium heat. Add the shallot, garlic and thyme or sage, and sauté until soft, about 5 minutes. Add the chicken livers and sauté for about 5 minutes until medium well-done. You want the livers to be mainly cooked, with a pink blush in the middle. Add the brandy and cook off the alcohol for a few minutes. I flambé the pan – sometimes this just happens by accident, so be prepared or you might lose your eyebrows!

Transfer the chicken liver mixture to a food processor and blitz until very smooth, scraping down the sides a few times with a spatula. Add the butter, one cube at a time, incorporating each cube fully before adding the next. With the motor running, add the cream in a very slow drizzle and process until the mixture is satiny smooth. If it starts to split, add a little more cream. Taste and season with salt and pepper – you want the pâté to be ever so slightly over-salted, as the salt flavour will reduce as it cools.

Spoon the mixture into the greased ramekins or large bowl. Bang firmly on the bench or a hard surface to level the pâté out and remove any air bubbles.

Recipe continued over page

Heat the pear paste and wine in a saucepan over a medium heat until the paste has dissolved. Mix well. Very carefully pour the liquid over the pâté to cover it completely. Place in the fridge to set, about an hour.

Serve with toasted bread and pickles, or on a platter with cornichons, lovely cheeses and meats such as prosciutto and salami. I've included some tasty dips, such as guacamole, tomato relish, pesto, babaganoush and hummus, in the basics section – these are also great on platters (see pages 208–215).

Serves 2–3

Prawn, lemon, pea and chilli spaghetti

Pasta is one of my great loves in life; sometimes I even have it with just butter, salt and pepper. This is a nice light pasta recipe without a sauce, and it's still packed with lots of fresh zingy flavour. With this dish in particular, I prefer using good old dried packet spaghetti. I like my pasta on the firmer side of al dente (which is how Italians would have it) and it's easier to get that result using dried pasta. You can choose which type you use!

200g dried spaghetti
1 tbsp olive oil
1 tbsp butter
3 cloves garlic, finely chopped
1 red chilli, deseeded and finely chopped
1½ cups raw prawns, deveined
1 cup firmly packed baby spinach leaves
1 cup cooked peas
1 cup ripe cherry tomatoes, halved
zest of 1 lemon
½ cup fresh grated parmesan
½ cup finely chopped fresh parsley leaves
handful basil leaves, ripped
1 tbsp good-quality olive oil
salt and freshly cracked black pepper
squeeze of lemon

Cook the spaghetti in plenty of salted water until just al dente. Drain and set aside.

Heat the olive oil and butter in a frying pan over a medium heat. Add the garlic and chilli and cook for about 5 minutes to soften, stirring frequently. Turn up the heat, add the prawns and sauté for a couple of minutes until only just cooked through.

Add the pasta to the pan along with the spinach, peas, cherry tomatoes, lemon zest, parmesan, and the herbs and olive oil. Stir to combine. Taste and season with salt and pepper.

Squeeze over some lemon juice and serve in bowls.

Serves 4

Greek-style lamb meatballs in pita pockets

Meatballs are one of my favourite things to make, and I don't like to stop at beef and spaghetti. Lamb mince is so tasty and lends itself perfectly to stronger flavours like these. I like making this as a filling lunch or a casual dinner – it's simple, healthy and a nice way to share a meal. In summer the meatballs are great done on the barbecue for a smoky flavour. Feel free to add some chopped up chillies to the sauce (or the patties) if you like a spicy kick.

Meatballs
500g lamb mince
½ onion, finely chopped
1 clove garlic, minced
2 tsp cumin seeds, toasted then lightly ground or bashed
1 slice wholemeal or white bread soaked in 1 tbsp milk
1 free-range egg, lightly beaten
salt and freshly cracked black pepper

Salad
1 red onion, thinly sliced
2 tsp salt
2 tomatoes, cored, deseeded and finely diced
1 cup cucumber, cored and finely diced
½ cup finely chopped fresh parsley leaves
1 tbsp extra virgin olive oil
1 tbsp lemon juice

Sauce
¾ cup unsweetened Greek yoghurt
1 clove garlic, minced
squeeze of lemon to taste

To cook and assemble
1 tbsp olive oil
100g feta, crumbled
½ iceberg lettuce, chopped
½ cup chopped fresh coriander or mint leaves
½ cup hummus (see page 212 or storebought)
5 large pita pockets, halved

Preheat the oven to 160°C.

Mix the lamb mince, onion, garlic, cumin seeds, bread and milk, and egg in a bowl with clean hands until well combined. Season generously with salt and pepper. Shape into walnut-sized meatballs. Place on a plate, cover and put in the fridge.

Arrange the red onion on a plate, and sprinkle the salt over the top. Leave to sit for 15–20 minutes, then rinse well and drain on paper towels. This removes the bitter taste. Mix the tomato, red onion, cucumber, parsley, olive oil and lemon juice together in a small bowl.

Mix the yoghurt with the garlic and squeeze of lemon juice.

Heat the olive oil in a frying pan over a medium-high heat and cook the meatballs in batches until browned all over. Drain on paper towels. Place the pita pockets in the oven for 5 minutes until slightly crispy.

Serve the meatballs, pita pockets, salad, yoghurt sauce, feta, lettuce, herbs and hummus in nice bowls on the table so everyone can help themselves and make their own tasty little pockets.

Serves 2–3

Haloumi and vege salad with capsicum dressing

Ah, haloumi, how I love you. If you haven't tried this cheese yet, you must – especially if you're a vegetarian! This is an amazing cheese which you can fry because of its high melting point: the outside goes golden and crispy and the inside gooey and delectable. What's more, it makes a pleasant squeaking sound when you chew it. Be sure to eat it as soon as possible after cooking it, as it will go rubbery when it cools down.

1 red capsicum, halved and deseeded
2–4 portobello mushrooms
2 courgettes, halved lengthways
1 red onion, quartered
4 whole cloves garlic, unpeeled
olive oil for cooking
salt and freshly cracked black pepper
¾ cup chopped chargrilled capsicum (see page 214 or storebought)
1 tbsp chopped fresh coriander leaves and stalks
¼ tsp ground cumin
1 tsp honey
1 tsp lemon juice
200g haloumi, cut into slices 1–2cm thick
fresh basil leaves to serve
crusty bread to serve

Preheat the oven to 180°C.

Place the capsicum, mushroom, courgette, onion quarters and garlic cloves in a roasting tray and drizzle with olive oil. Toss well to coat everything, and season with salt and pepper. Bake in the oven for 20 minutes or until cooked through.

Place the chargrilled capsicum, coriander, cumin and honey in a food processor. Squeeze the garlic cloves from their skins into the processor. Process until well mixed. Taste and add the lemon juice, and season with salt and pepper.

Heat a little olive oil in a frying pan over a medium-high heat. Add the haloumi slices and cook for a few minutes until golden brown on both sides. Drain on paper towels.

Place the roasted mushrooms on two plates. Arrange the capsicum, courgette, haloumi and onion on top. Top with the basil. Drizzle the capsicum dressing on top and serve with crusty bread.

Serves 2–3 as lunch or an entrée

Smoked fish niçoise

My family summers largely revolved around fishing, and I don't think there was a more enthusiastic fisherkid than me. If we were lucky enough to bag a kahawai or trevally from a trawl, we'd be enjoying fresh home-smoked fish soon after. Here, I've used it in my take on a niçoise salad. Sadly, I don't live by the seaside with a limitless supply of fish, so it's handy that smoked fish is now relatively inexpensive! Serve this with grilled bread.

Vinaigrette

3 anchovy fillets
3 tbsp extra virgin olive oil
1 clove garlic, roughly chopped
1 tbsp mayonnaise
1 tbsp lemon juice
2 tsp chopped fresh dill
1 tsp Dijon mustard
salt and freshly cracked black pepper

Salad

1 tbsp capers
olive oil for cooking
500g baby new potatoes, skin on, halved or quartered
250g green beans
300–400g good-quality smoked fish, skin and bones removed, roughly flaked into chunks
½ red onion, sliced
½ cup kalamata olives
1 cos lettuce
6 ripe truss tomatoes, cored and quartered
3–4 hard-boiled free-range eggs, halved

To make the vinaigrette, process all the ingredients in a food processor until smooth. Taste and adjust seasoning.

To prepare the salad, fry the capers in a small frying pan with a little olive oil until crispy and puffy.

Cook the potatoes in salted boiling water until tender. Drain and cool slightly.

Blanch the green beans in boiling water for a few minutes until al dente, then refresh under cold water. Drain and set aside.

Put the fish, potatoes, beans, onion, olives and lettuce leaves in a large mixing bowl. Add half the dressing and mix very gently to coat. Arrange the salad on a serving plate, and top with the tomatoes, capers and hard-boiled eggs. Drizzle with the remaining dressing.

Serves 2–3

Kumara and asparagus salad

Forget the sad, limp 1980s-style potato and pasta salads from days of old, because you have your new summer barbecue salad staple right here. It's fresh, healthy and delicious, and the leftovers will be a welcome treat in someone's packed lunch the day after. When asparagus isn't in season, you can use green beans instead.

Dressing

2 tbsp extra virgin olive oil
2 tbsp lemon juice
1 tsp sugar
1 tsp wholegrain mustard
salt and freshly cracked black pepper

Salad

1kg kumara, peeled and cut into 6cm pieces
olive oil for cooking
salt and freshly cracked black pepper
1–2 bunches fresh asparagus, hard ends snapped off
¾ cup walnut pieces
½ red onion, thinly sliced
1 spring onion, chopped
1 tbsp finely chopped fresh parsley leaves
1 tbsp finely chopped fresh basil leaves
1 cup croutons (see page 178)

Preheat the oven to 180°C.

To make the dressing, whisk all the ingredients together in a small bowl until combined.

Place the kumara in a roasting tray, coat in a little olive oil, and season with salt and pepper. Bake in the oven for 20 minutes or until golden and cooked through. Cool.

Blanch the asparagus in boiling water for a couple of minutes until tender but still al dente. Drain and set aside.

Put the kumara, asparagus, walnuts, red onion, spring onion and the parsley and basil in a bowl. Add the dressing and mix gently to coat. Taste and season with salt and pepper. Sprinkle with the croutons and serve.

Serves 2 as an entrée or 4 as a nibble

Tricolore salad with reduced balsamic

This salad is simple to make, beautiful to look at, and fresh and lovely to eat. It reminds me of long summers in the sun. I was lucky enough to go to Italy a few years back and this dish was a staple with a nice glass of pinot grigio at sunset!

The success of this dish relies heavily on the quality of the ingredients, so only use fresh mozzarella and make sure the tomatoes are red, ripe and juicy (cherry tomatoes are nice to use, too). You could also add some thinly sliced prosciutto for a salty bite.

½ cup balsamic vinegar
8–9 ripe truss tomatoes, sliced
1 x 250g tub fresh buffalo mozzarella, drained
1 cup fresh basil leaves
salt and freshly cracked black pepper
good-quality extra virgin olive oil to serve

Heat the balsamic vinegar in a small saucepan over a low heat, and simmer very gently until it has reduced and thickened to a syrup-like consistency. Set aside.

Place the tomato slices on a platter. If the mozzarella balls are large, slice into pieces. Arrange on the tomato slices, then top with the basil leaves. Season with salt and pepper. Drizzle with the reduced balsamic and a little olive oil.

Serves 3–4

Bacon, pumpkin and chickpea salad with feta dressing

This salad is robust, tasty and filling. I used to make a big batch of it at the start of the week and take it to work for healthy, delicious lunches, but you can serve it with bread, or as a side dish with a meal or at a barbecue. Get creative and try adding different things – check what you have in the vege drawers of your fridge. If you're vegetarian, omit the bacon and add something else for an extra bit of crunch, such as ciabatta croutons or celery.

Dressing

1 clove garlic, chopped
1 tbsp chopped fresh coriander leaves and stalks
2 tbsp crumbled feta
1 tbsp white wine vinegar
1 tsp sugar
3 tbsp extra virgin olive oil
salt and freshly cracked black pepper

Salad

500g pumpkin, cut into 6cm pieces
5 whole cloves garlic, unpeeled
1 tbsp extra virgin olive oil
1½ cups chopped bacon
1½ cups baby spinach leaves
1 x 420g can chickpeas, drained and rinsed
4–5 fresh basil leaves, ripped
¼ cup fresh coriander leaves
¼ cup sango sprouts or microgreens

Preheat the oven to 180°C.

To make the dressing, process all the ingredients in a food processor until smooth and creamy. Or chop the garlic and coriander very finely and mix with the rest of the ingredients by hand with a whisk. Taste and adjust seasoning.

To prepare the salad, place the pumpkin pieces in a roasting tray with the whole garlic, drizzle with the olive oil and toss to coat. Season with salt and pepper. Bake in the oven for 30–40 minutes or until the pumpkin is cooked through.

Fry the bacon in a frying pan over a medium-high heat until very crispy. Drain well on paper towels.

Place the warm pumpkin, bacon, baby spinach leaves, chickpeas, basil and coriander in a large bowl. Squeeze the roasted garlic out of its skin into the bowl. Season with a little salt and pepper, and mix well to combine.

Drizzle with the dressing, then sprinkle with the sango sprouts or microgreens.

Serves 5–6

Soul chicken and vegetable soup

I love making my own chicken stock – it tastes better, it probably costs less overall, and it's so satisfying. After you've cooked the chook, used the meat for the soup, and given the skin and gristle to the dog, you are only left with a tiny pile of clean bones. No waste – massive taste! And the cooking stock fills the house with a beautiful, soulful smell, too.

This soup is even better reheated the next day. Just to warn you, though, it may solidify into a strange-looking jelly in the fridge; this is just the good protein in the stock, nothing to be worried about. It will turn back into a liquid as soon as you reheat it.

Stock

1 size 14 whole chicken, quartered
1½ litres water
1 onion, roughly chopped
2 stalks celery, including leaves
1 large or 2 small carrots, roughly chopped
1 leek, white part only, roughly chopped
8 whole peppercorns
1 bay leaf
1 tsp vegetable stock powder

Soup

2 stalks celery, chopped
1 carrot, diced
1 cup chopped cauliflower florets
1 cup fresh, frozen or canned corn kernels
1 cup macaroni or broken-up pasta of your choice (I use fettuccine which I wrap in a tea towel and break into pieces by sliding it down against a table edge)
½ tsp cayenne pepper (optional)
salt and freshly cracked black pepper

Place all the stock ingredients, including the entire chicken – ribcage and all – in a stock pot, cover and simmer over a low heat for 1½ hours (do not boil). Remove the chicken and set aside. Strain everything else through a colander, mashing as much juice out of the veges as possible. You can also strain it through a sieve if you like. Reserve any bits of chicken and discard everything else.

Wait for the broth to cool a little, then skim most of the fat off the surface. It's okay to leave a little there for flavour.

Pick the flesh from the chicken bones and add it back into the broth in the pot. Add the vegetables, pasta and cayenne pepper if using. Bring to a simmer and cook until the vegetables are just tender. Taste and season with salt and pepper.

Serve with crispy garlic bread or buttered toast.

Serves 4–6

Leek and potato soup with gruyère crust

This lovely, comforting soup is inexpensive to make and it tastes just as comforting and satisfying as it looks. The crunchy pieces of gruyère toast add texture and a nice nutty flavour to the dish. If you are vegetarian, use vegetable stock instead of chicken. If you have a herb garden, add whatever blend of soft herbs you are growing as a garnish for a hit of fresh flavours.

1 tbsp olive oil
1 onion, finely chopped
1 shallot, finely chopped
2 cloves garlic, chopped
2 tsp chopped fresh thyme leaves
1 tsp finely chopped fresh rosemary leaves
1kg potatoes, peeled and cut into 5cm pieces
3 cups chicken or vegetable stock
2 leeks, white part only, sliced
½ cup chopped fresh chives
½ cup chopped fresh flat-leaf parsley leaves
salt and freshly cracked black pepper

3–4 slices fresh bread
3–4 slices gruyère

Heat the olive oil in a large saucepan over a medium heat. Add the onion, shallot, garlic, thyme and rosemary, and cook for around 5 minutes until soft. Add the potato pieces and stock, cover and then simmer for around 20 minutes until the potato is tender. Mash roughly with a wooden spoon to break up the potatoes a little. Add the leek, stir to combine and cook until the leek is just tender, around 10 minutes. Add half the chives and parsley, and stir. Taste and season with salt and pepper.

Preheat the grill to 200°C.

Grill the bread on one side and then turn over and top the uncooked side with a slice or two of gruyère. Place back under the grill for a few minutes until the cheese is bubbling and golden and the bread is crunchy.

Serve the soup in bowls, and add a whole or half a slice of cheesy bread into each serving of soup. Then sprinkle with the remaining chives and parsley.

Serves 3–4

Mushroom soup with buttery garlic mushroom toppers

The great thing about this soup is that you get exactly what you sign up for – a lovely silky soup that sings with rich, vibrant mushroom flavour. When I was creating this recipe, I was reminded that sometimes less is more. Everything in this recipe is used only to enhance the natural flavour of the hero ingredient. It's simple and absolutely delicious.

Soup

25g butter
1 tbsp extra virgin olive oil
1 onion, chopped
1 shallot, chopped
2 cloves garlic, chopped
2 tsp chopped fresh thyme leaves
5–6 fresh sage leaves, chopped
600g brown button mushrooms, sliced
2 cups chicken or vegetable stock
½ cup cream
¼ tsp white pepper
salt and freshly cracked black pepper

Toppers

1½ cups day-old bread, cut into small pieces
25g butter, softened
1 tbsp finely chopped fresh parsley leaves
2 cloves garlic, minced
4 large portobello mushrooms, stems removed

cream to serve
fresh parsley leaves to serve

Preheat the oven to 220°C. Line a baking tray with baking paper.

Melt the butter with the oil in a large saucepan over a medium heat. Add the onion, shallot, garlic, thyme and sage leaves, and sauté for 5 minutes until soft. Add the mushrooms and cook for another few minutes. Add the stock and simmer gently for 15–20 minutes until the mushrooms are soft. Add the cream and white pepper. Use a stick blender or transfer to a blender to purée the mixture to a silky smooth soup. Return to the stovetop briefly to reheat before serving. Taste and season with salt and black pepper.

Meanwhile, make the toppers. Mix the bread, butter, parsley and garlic until well combined. Season with a little salt and black pepper. Place the mushrooms upside down on the prepared tray and top with a pile of the garlicky bread.

Roast in the oven for 7–10 minutes until the bread is crunchy and the mushrooms cooked through.

Serve the soup with a mushroom topper, a swirl of cream and a sprinkling of parsley leaves.

Serves 6–8

Pea and ham soup

Everyone probably has a pea soup recipe they think is the best one ever, so I realise I'm being a little bold to put one in my cookbook. This recipe is world famous among our extended family and friends. It's my oma's old recipe, affectionately known as 'Oma Soup' to one and all. It's hearty, packed with flavour, full of natural goodness and absolutely delicious. I'm so happy to share the recipe with you (I know Oma would be, too), and I hope your family enjoys it as much as mine does.

Stock

1 smoked bacon hock (choose the biggest one)
1 onion, roughly chopped
1 bay leaf
3 carrots, roughly chopped
4 whole peppercorns
4 litres water

Soup

1½ cups vegetable stock
1 x 450g packet (2 cups) split green peas
1 cup red lentils
1 leek, white part only, thinly sliced
1 bunch celery, including leaves, chopped
2 large carrots, grated
2 tsp vegetable stock powder
salt and freshly cracked black pepper
crusty bread to serve

Place the bacon hock, onion, bay leaf, chopped carrots, peppercorns and water in a large stock pot. Cover and simmer for 2–3 hours or until the meat falls off the bone. Gently remove the pork hock and any meat that has fallen off, and set aside. Strain the cooking liquid, reserving it, and discard the vegetables.

When the pork hock is cool, remove the good meat from the bone and chop it into small pieces. Set the chopped meat aside and discard the bones, skin and cartilage.

Put the broth back into the rinsed pot, along with the stock. Add the split peas and lentils, and simmer for 30 minutes or until the peas are soft. Add the meat, leek, celery, grated carrot and stock powder, and cook until the veges are tender, about 30 minutes. Taste and season well with salt and pepper.

Serve with crusty buttered bread.

Serves 4–6

Tomato and meatball soup

In summer when tomatoes are in abundance (and affordable!), I'll use fresh ones for this recipe, but in winter it's perfectly fine to use canned – the soup will taste just as good. You can leave out the meatballs for a vegetarian option and you'll still have a very tasty tomato soup.

Meatballs
500g beef mince
1 free-range egg, lightly beaten
1 slice bread soaked in 1 tbsp milk
½ tsp ground cumin
1 clove garlic, finely chopped
¼ tsp salt
freshly cracked black pepper
1 tbsp olive oil

Soup
1 tbsp olive oil
2 onions, chopped
1 clove garlic, chopped
4 stalks celery, chopped
3 cups vegetable or salt-reduced chicken stock
12–15 large ripe tomatoes, cored and chopped, or 4 x 400g cans chopped tomatoes
1 large potato, peeled and chopped into 1cm dice
3–4 tsp sugar
1 slice wholemeal bread, torn into chunks
¼ cup cream, plus extra for serving
¼ cup chopped fresh flat-leaf parsley leaves, plus extra for serving

To make the meatballs, combine all the ingredients except the olive oil in a bowl and mix well to combine. Roll into walnut-sized balls.

Heat the oil in a frying pan over a high heat and fry the meatballs in batches until golden all over. Drain on paper towels and set aside.

To make the soup, heat the oil in a large saucepan over a medium heat. Add the onion, garlic and celery, and cook for 5 minutes until soft. Add the stock, tomatoes, potato and sugar, and simmer for 30 minutes or until the potato is tender. Add the bread and stir through. Purèe the soup using a stick blender or transfer to a food processor or blender, and blend until smooth. Taste and season with salt and pepper. You can add a little more stock here if you prefer a thinner soup.

Return to the stovetop, add the cream and meatballs, and simmer for a few minutes to heat the meatballs through. Stir in the parsley.

Serve in soup bowls with a swirl of cream and a sprinkle of chopped parsley.

Serves 6–8

Quiche Lorraine

This is my take on a classic-style quiche, and I love the wonderfully simple yet perfect flavours of the bacon, garlic, leek and creamy egg and the crispy pastry shell. It works as a lunch, a light dinner or to take along to a summer picnic. Serve it hot or cold with a zingy, leafy little salad and some chutney. The leftover slices are still so tasty the next day as a special treat in a lunchbox.

1–2 sheets shortcrust savoury pastry (or make your own)
25g butter
4 rashers bacon, finely chopped
1 leek, white part only, cut into 1cm dice
¼ cup dry white wine
6 free-range eggs
½ cup cream
½ cup milk
1 tsp Dijon mustard
2 tsp chopped fresh thyme leaves
1 tbsp very finely chopped fresh parsley leaves
pinch salt
¼ tsp white pepper
½ cup grated gruyére

Preheat the oven to 180°C. Grease a 28cm flan or tart dish.

Line the flan or tart dish with the pastry. Trim the pastry with a knife so the edges are nice and neat. Prick the bottom with a fork about 10 times. Cut a round of baking paper to fit the base and sides of the dish. Place the baking paper on top of the pastry, and cover with baking beads or rice. Bake in the oven for 10 minutes, then remove the paper and baking beads, and bake for another 5 minutes. Remove from the oven.

Melt the butter in a pan over a high heat. Add the bacon and sauté for 5 minutes until it starts to crisp up. Add the leek and cook for a few more minutes until soft. Add the white wine and simmer until the liquid has almost evaporated. Set aside.

Whisk together the eggs, cream, milk, mustard, thyme leaves, parsley, salt and white pepper until well combined. Add the cheese and stir to combine. Stir in the leek and bacon mixture.

Pour the filling into the pastry case and bake in the oven for 15–20 minutes or until the middle still has a very slight wobble. Remove from the oven and cool in the dish.

Serves 6–8

Roasted pumpkin, beetroot and goat's cheese quiche

This great quiche is vibrant and colourful, packed with great flavours and loaded with lots of healthy veges. I wrote the recipe with my sister in mind, and used fresh eggs from Mum's farm – so this one is dear to my heart! My mum always made her own pastry for quiches and pies using wholemeal flour, so the end result was a very healthy meal. If you prefer to make your own pastry, then please do. If you're not a fan of goat's cheese, you can use feta instead.

2 small or 1 large beetroot, unpeeled
olive oil for cooking
2 cups chopped pumpkin, cut into 2cm dice
2 sheets savoury shortcrust pastry (or make your own)
5 free-range eggs
½ cup cream
¼ cup freshly grated parmesan
1 tsp salt
freshly cracked black pepper
½ onion, finely chopped
2 cups finely chopped spinach, washed and excess moisture squeezed out
1 chargrilled red capsicum, sliced into strips (see page 214 or storebought)
1 bunch asparagus or 3 courgettes, chopped
50g soft goat's cheese
¼ cup pumpkin seeds
½ tsp cumin seeds

Preheat the oven to 180°C. Grease a 28cm quiche or flan dish, and line the base with baking paper.

Wrap the beetroot in foil and roast in the oven for 40–50 minutes. Halfway through, add the pumpkin pieces drizzled with olive oil, in a roasting tray. Remove the skins when cool and set aside.

Line the quiche or flan dish with the pastry, trimming the pastry edges. Prick holes in the base with a fork. Cut a piece of baking paper to fit the base and sides of the dish. Place the baking paper on the pastry and fill with rice or baking beads. Bake for 10 minutes, then remove the rice or beads and paper. Return the pastry base to the oven for a further 5 minutes.

Put the eggs in a bowl with the cream, parmesan, salt and pepper, and beat to fully incorporate the egg.

Arrange the pumpkin and beetroot pieces on the pastry base. Sprinkle over the onion, then cover with the spinach. Pour the cream mixture over everything. Arrange the sliced red capsicum and asparagus or courgettes nicely on top. Crumble over the goat's cheese, then sprinkle with the pumpkin and cumin seeds. Add another good crack of pepper.

Bake in the oven for 30 minutes or until golden and the vegetables are cooked through.

Serve with a nice tomato relish (see page 213).

Chapter four

Burgers

A good homemade burger is a thing of beauty, and certainly nothing to be afraid of. (Unlike the ones from a fast-food joint – we should be scared of those!) As with any food, as long as you use good-quality ingredients that work well together and quality condiments, you can't really go wrong. While a well-made mince pattie is always going to be a firm favourite with me, I do like to experiment with different styles of burger fillings. I've put all my favourites in here for you to try. For the filling ingredients, use as much as you need or want based on how many people you are serving.

For the actual burger buns, I like to mix it up each time. There is a great range of buns around that you can try – sliders, sourdough rolls, wholemeal and grainy buns, baps, or even some lovely Turkish pide buns. Check out what your local bakery has to offer next time you're there. Texturally and flavour-wise, they'll be a lot nicer than the plain white burger buns at the supermarket.

Serves 4

Cajun chicken burgers with avocado and mayo

Making your own Cajun seasoning is an easy way to add an interesting twist to chicken – it works beautifully here in a burger with the creamy avocado mayo.

Marinade

½ cup finely diced white onion
2 cloves garlic, finely chopped
1 tsp dried oregano
1 tsp dried thyme
1 tsp dried basil
½ tsp smoked or plain paprika
½ tsp cayenne pepper
½ tsp brown sugar
¼ tsp salt
freshly cracked black pepper
5 boneless, skinless chicken thighs
1 tbsp olive oil

To assemble

4–6 ciabatta or burger buns
6 slices cheese
baby cos lettuce leaves
tomato slices
sliced red onion
fresh basil leaves
1 avocado, mashed
homemade mayonnaise or aïoli (see page 210 or use good storebought)

Combine all the marinade ingredients except the chicken and olive oil. Add the chicken thighs and toss to coat evenly. Cover and marinate in the fridge for at least an hour.

Heat the olive oil in a frying pan over a high heat. Add the thighs and cook, turning, until the chicken is cooked through.

Preheat the grill to 200°C.

Place all the bun halves on a baking tray, and place a slice of cheese on the bottom half of each bun. Grill the buns for a few minutes until slightly crispy and the cheese has melted.

Divide the chicken among the bases, then follow with the lettuce, tomato, red onion and basil. Spread the top of each bun generously with the avocado and mayonnaise, and place on top of the burger. Dig in and enjoy!

Serves 4

Barbecued chicken burgers

If you want to eat these on a rainy old winter's day, just use a standard frying pan.

3–4 boneless, skinless chicken breasts, halved horizontally
½ cup finely chopped fresh coriander leaves and stalks
2 tbsp chopped fresh parsley leaves
1 tbsp lemon juice
zest of 1 lemon
2 tbsp olive oil
pinch chilli flakes (optional)
½ tsp salt
freshly cracked black pepper
oil for cooking

To assemble

½ cup mayonnaise (see page 210 or use good storebought)
1 clove garlic, finely chopped
⅓ cup crumbled feta
½ cup or a handful fresh basil leaves
6 ciabatta or burger buns
10–12 slices cheddar cheese
baby spinach leaves
cucumber ribbons
sliced red onion
grilled bacon (optional)

Place the chicken in a bowl with the coriander, parsley, lemon juice and zest, oil and chilli flakes if using, salt and a good crack of pepper. Mix well to combine. If you have time, marinate in the fridge for at least 20 minutes to an hour.

Heat a little oil on a barbecue grill, or in a grill pan over a high heat, add the chicken and cook, turning, until cooked through.

Process the mayonnaise, garlic, feta and basil leaves in a food processor until combined (or chop the basil finely and mix with the other ingredients). Taste and season with salt and pepper.

Preheat the grill to 200°C.

Place all the bun halves on a baking tray, and place a few slices of cheese on the bottom half of each bun. Grill the buns for a few minutes until slightly crispy and the cheese has melted.

Divide the chicken among the bun bases, then follow with the other ingredients. Spread the top of each bun generously with the herb mayonnaise, and place on top of the burger. Dig in and enjoy!

Serves 4

Fresh salmon burgers

This is taking burgers to a whole new level of sophistication! Not only is this recipe lip-smackingly good, it's a nice way to make a couple of salmon fillets stretch out for a family. The patties will seem extremely soft when you're forming them, but they will hold together as they cook. Make sure you squeeze a little lemon onto the patties after cooking, to add a fresh zing (not before or the fish will start to cook in the bowl).

600–700g fresh salmon, skin and bones removed, very finely chopped
½ red onion, very finely chopped
2 tsp capers
2 tsp chopped fresh dill
1 tsp very finely chopped fresh parsley leaves
1 tsp Dijon mustard
1 free-range egg white, lightly beaten
2 tsp lemon zest
pinch chilli flakes (optional)
¼ tsp salt
freshly cracked black pepper
flour for dusting
olive oil for cooking

To assemble

4–6 ciabatta or burger buns
squeeze of lemon
tartare sauce or mayonnaise (see page 210–211 or use good storebought)
sliced gherkins
sliced cucumber
fresh basil leaves
lettuce or spinach leaves

Place the salmon in a bowl with the onion, capers, dill, parsley, mustard, egg white, lemon zest, chilli flakes if using, salt and pepper. Carefully shape into 4 large or 5–6 smaller patties. The mixture will appear to be quite soft and hard to shape, but the egg white will set the patties.

Put some flour on a plate and carefully dust each pattie. Place on a plate, cover and pop in the fridge for 15–20 minutes.

Heat a little olive oil in a large frying pan over a medium-high heat. Add the patties, and cook for a few minutes each side, turning carefully. Be careful not to overcook the fish.

Preheat the grill to 200°C.

Cut the buns in half and place on a baking tray. Grill the buns for a few minutes until slightly crispy.

Serve the patties on the grilled buns, squeeze over a little lemon juice and follow with the tartare sauce or mayonnaise, gherkins, cucumber, basil and lettuce or spinach leaves.

Serves 4

Steak and bacon sandwiches with smoky mayo and crispy onion rings

This is what I call a beefed-up, bloke-pleasing burger! Look at it – pretty mouthwatering, even if I do say so myself. The smoked paprika adds a delicious smoky barbecue flavour to the mayonnaise, and when combined with juicy steak, cheese, onion rings and bacon, suddenly you have a fantastic meal that will put you in the good books for a long time!

Onion rings

neutral oil for deep-frying (rice bran or canola)
1¼ cups self-raising flour
1 tsp salt
2 onions, sliced into 2cm rings
1 free-range egg
1 cup milk, approximately

To cook and assemble

½ cup mayonnaise (see page 210 or use good storebought)
½–1 tsp smoked paprika
600–800g steak (I use sirloin)
olive oil for cooking
salt and freshly ground black pepper
4–5 bread rolls or burger buns (I use Turkish buns)
6–7 cheddar cheese slices
cherry tomatoes or tomato slices
lettuce leaves
hot English mustard
tomato relish (see page 213)
grilled bacon rashers (optional)

To make the onion rings, heat a good amount of oil in a saucepan over a medium-high heat to 185°C. Dip in the end of a wooden spoon to test the heat – if bubbles form around it, then the oil is ready.

Stir the flour and salt together in a small bowl. Dip the rings into the flour mixture to coat and set aside on a plate. Whisk the egg and milk into the flour mixture to form a smooth batter. Dip the floured rings into the batter to coat, then place on a wire rack with baking paper underneath for a few minutes until the batter stops dripping.

Fry the rings, in batches, for a minute or so each side or until golden brown all over. Drain on paper towels. Sprinkle with a little salt and set aside.

Mix the mayonnaise and smoked paprika in a bowl and set aside. If you like, lightly flatten the steaks with a meat mallet or rolling pin – this will allow for quicker cooking and you might be able to cut each steak in half for two 'patties'.

Heat a little olive oil in a frying pan or on a barbecue grill plate over a high heat. Season the steak with salt and pepper and cook for 1–2 minutes on each side until medium-rare. Set aside on a plate to rest for 10 minutes, then slice.

Preheat the grill to 200°C.

Place the bun halves on a baking tray, with a few slices of cheese on the bun bases. Butter the bun tops. Bake in the oven for a couple of minutes until the cheese is melted and the buns crispy.

Serve the steak on the buns with the onion rings, smoky mayo and other accompaniments.

Serves 4

Tandoori-style chicken burgers

I made these on the spur of the moment for a good friend who dropped around for lunch one day. She loved it so much I had to write down the recipe for her right then and there, so she could make it again for dinner that night! The chicken is fabulous done on the barbecue if the weather's right, as tandoori chicken is meant to have a slight char on the outside. A normal oven will also work just fine, though.

Chicken

6–8 boneless, skinless chicken thighs or breasts
1 tbsp olive oil
⅔ cup plain unsweetened yoghurt
2 cloves garlic, finely chopped
2 tsp grated fresh ginger
1 tbsp lemon juice
1 tsp garam masala
1 tsp ground coriander
1 tsp ground cumin
½ tsp chilli powder
½ tsp ground turmeric
½ tsp salt

To assemble

4–6 burger buns
peach chutney (storebought)
tomato relish (see page 213)
lettuce leaves
plain unsweetened yoghurt
chopped fresh coriander leaves
chopped fresh mint leaves
sliced red onion
salt and freshly cracked black pepper

Preheat the grill to high.

Place the chicken thighs or breasts between two sheets of cling film and whack with a rolling pin or a meat mallet to even them out. Cut a few slits 1cm deep in the top of each chicken thigh or breast. Mix all the remaining tandoori chicken ingredients together in a roasting tray. Add the chicken pieces and coat in the marinade. Cover and marinate in the fridge for 20–30 minutes.

Place the chicken under the grill for 5–10 minutes on each side until brown, even a little charred. Turn the oven down to 180°C and change the setting to bake. Move the tray to the middle of the oven and cook for another 5–10 minutes or until the chicken is cooked through.

Increase the oven temperature to 200°C and change the setting back to grill.

Cut the buns in half and place on a baking tray. Grill the buns for a few minutes until slightly crispy.

Divide the chicken among the grilled buns and follow with the chutney, relish, lettuce, yoghurt, fresh herbs and onion, and season with salt and pepper.

Chapter five
Pizza

Biting into a slice of well-made pizza is one of life's great pleasures. And forget about the stodgy, oily pizzas that flop out of fast-food joints – you can do much better in your own kitchen.

Once you've mastered the dough, you're away laughing and you can freeze a few dough balls to whip out whenever you want a super-quick meal. You can experiment and get fairly imaginative with the toppings. Take a look at what you have in your fridge, think about the different elements and taste them in your mind.

To cook the pizzas, you can use a plain baking tray (which works fine), a metal pizza pan, a perforated pizza pan, a pizza stone, or just build a pizza oven in your backyard (I can dream).

If you use a pizza stone, be sure to preheat it in the hot oven first, and flour it well. Baking trays and pizza pans need to be greased well to avoid the pizza sticking.

Makes about 2 cups

Pizza sauce

This pizza sauce is delicious, and pretty versatile – if you have some left over, you could toss it through some pasta or use it like relish on a sandwich.

olive oil for cooking
½ onion, finely chopped
1 clove garlic, finely chopped
1 tbsp tomato paste
1 x 400g can chopped tomatoes
1 tsp sugar
1 tsp vinegar
salt and freshly cracked black pepper
¼ cup chopped fresh basil leaves

Heat a splash of olive oil in a frying pan over a medium heat. Add the onion, garlic and tomato paste and sauté for 3–5 minutes until the onion is soft. Add the tomatoes, sugar and vinegar. Turn down the heat, stir and simmer gently for 15–20 minutes until reduced to a nice thick sauce.

You can either use it as it is or purée for a smoother texture – it's up to you. Taste and season with salt and pepper. Stir through the fresh basil.

Makes enough for 5–6 pizzas

Pizza dough

1½ cups warm water
1 tsp sugar
2 tsp dried yeast
4 cups plain flour
1 tsp salt
¼ cup extra virgin olive oil

Whisk the warm water, sugar and yeast together in a bowl until well combined. Set aside for 5 minutes or until the mixture foams – this is the yeast activating.

Sift the flour into a bowl with the salt. Make a well in the centre, and pour in the yeast mixture and olive oil. Use a spatula to bring the mixture together from the centre in a brisk stirring motion, then use clean hands to form a soft dough.

Place the dough ball on a lightly floured surface and knead for around 10 minutes – the dough should end up very stretchy and smooth. Place the dough in a large oiled bowl, cut a criss-cross shape in the top, cover with cling film, and set aside in a warm place (such as the hot water cupboard or in front of the heater) for 30 minutes, or until the dough has doubled in size – hence the need for a big bowl. The ideal temperature is 21–25°C.

Punch down the risen dough a couple of times, just to knock the air out of it. Divide the dough into balls, depending on how many pizzas you want. The dough can be placed in ziplock bags and frozen at this point.

Roll out and top with your favourite toppings.

Serves 4

Chilli, olive and tomato pizza

You can make this pizza as hot as you like! If you like a milder pizza remove the seeds from the fresh chillies first. If you can't find fresh ones, then dried chilli will work as well.

1 quantity pizza dough (see page 103 or use Turkish pizza bases)
½ cup pizza sauce (see page 102)
2 cloves garlic, finely chopped
handful baby spinach leaves
handful freshly grated parmesan
3–4 ripe tomatoes, sliced
handful kalamata olives
a few capers
a few anchovy fillets, chopped (optional)
1–2 red chillies, chopped
salt and freshly cracked black pepper
baby spinach leaves dressed with a little extra virgin olive oil to serve

Preheat the oven to 220°C fan-bake (or as hot as your oven will go). Place your pizza stone or baking tray in the centre of the oven to heat up.

Roll out a portion of pizza dough on a clean floured benchtop to your desired pizza size, then place on a clean, dry baking tray dusted with a good amount of semolina or flour to prevent the pizza sticking.

Spread the sauce over the base and sprinkle with garlic. Scatter over a layer of baby spinach leaves, then a handful of grated parmesan. Top with the tomatoes, olives, capers, anchovies if using, and chilli, depending on how hot you like it. Season with salt and pepper.

Carefully transfer the pizza to the preheated pizza stone or baking tray, and replace in the centre of the oven. Cook until the pizza base is crispy – about 10–12 minutes with a pizza stone or 15–18 minutes on a tray.

Remove from the oven, place a pile of spinach leaves on top and serve.

Serves 4

Greek lamb pizza

This is a great way to make a little lamb go a long way! This pizza is packed with flavour and the yoghurt and mint sauce adds a lovely fresh finish.

500g diced lamb
olive oil for cooking
½ tsp ground cumin
¼ tsp ground cardamom
½ tsp salt
1 cup plain unsweetened yoghurt
½ cup finely chopped fresh mint leaves
2 tsp lemon juice
salt and freshly cracked black pepper
1 quantity pizza dough (see page 103 or use Turkish pizza bases)
½ cup pizza sauce (see page 102)
2 cloves garlic, chopped
1 cup ripe cherry tomatoes, halved or tomatoes, cored and quartered
½ red onion, sliced
pinch chilli flakes
handful chopped fresh mint leaves to serve

Preheat the oven to 220°C fan-bake (or as hot as your oven will go). Place your pizza stone or baking tray in the centre of the oven to heat up.

Coat the lamb pieces in a little olive oil in a bowl. Add the cumin, cardamom and salt, and mix well to combine. Set aside for the flavours to infuse.

Mix the yoghurt, mint and lemon juice together, and season with a little salt and pepper.

Heat a little olive oil in a frying pan over a high heat. Add the lamb pieces and sear for a few minutes until golden brown. Set aside.

Roll out a portion of the pizza dough on a clean floured benchtop to your desired pizza size, then place on a clean, dry baking tray dusted with a good amount of semolina or flour to prevent the pizza sticking. Spread the sauce on the base and sprinkle with the garlic. Add the cooked lamb pieces, tomato, onion and chilli flakes. Season with salt and pepper.

Carefully transfer the pizza to the preheated pizza stone or baking tray, and replace in the centre of the oven. Cook until the pizza base is crispy – about 10–12 minutes with a pizza stone or 15–18 minutes on a tray.

Remove from the oven, sprinkle with the chopped mint and drizzle with the yoghurt sauce.

Serves 4

Prawn, garlic and aïoli pizza

This is a pizza my girlfriends and I whip together when we're catching up over a glass of wine. It's just so tasty, and it's nice and light to eat, depending on how much aïoli you drizzle on top. For a bit of extra colour, you could scatter some baby spinach leaves on top as well.

1 quantity pizza dough (see page 103 or use Turkish pizza bases)
¾ cup pizza sauce (see page 102)
3–4 cloves garlic, finely chopped
handful grated mozzarella
400g raw prawns, shelled, deveined and tails removed
1 red onion, sliced
1 red capsicum, cored, deseeded and thinly sliced
salt and freshly cracked black pepper
extra virgin olive oil for brushing
aïoli (see page 210 or use good storebought)
squeeze of lemon
fresh dill sprigs to garnish

Preheat the oven to 220°C fan-bake (or as hot as your oven will go). Place your pizza stone or baking tray in the centre of the oven to heat up.

Roll out a portion of pizza dough on a clean floured benchtop to your desired pizza size, then place on a clean, dry baking tray dusted with a good amount of semolina or flour to prevent the pizza sticking.

Spread the sauce over the base and sprinkle with the garlic. Scatter over a layer of mozzarella. Add the prawns, onion and capsicum. Season with salt and pepper. Brush the edges of the pizza with a little olive oil.

Carefully transfer the pizza to the preheated pizza stone or baking tray, and replace in the centre of the oven. Cook until the pizza base is crispy – about 10–12 minutes with a pizza stone or 15–18 minutes on a tray.

Remove from the oven and drizzle the pizza with aïoli, squeeze over some lemon juice and sprinkle with the fresh dill.

Serves 4

Prosciutto, mozzarella and basil pizza

This pizza is one of my all-time favourites – simple, fresh, colourful and tasty. Add a nice whack of salt and a splash of balsamic, and you're in pizza heaven.

1 quantity pizza dough (see page 103 or use Turkish pizza bases)
¾ cup pizza sauce (see page 102)
1–2 cloves garlic, finely chopped
handful freshly grated parmesan
3–4 fresh ripe tomatoes, topped and sliced
1–2 large balls fresh mozzarella, sliced
extra virgin olive oil for brushing
salt and freshly cracked black pepper
5–6 slices prosciutto
handful fresh basil leaves
good-quality balsamic vinegar for drizzling (optional)

Preheat the oven to 220°C fan-bake (or as hot as your oven will go). Place your pizza stone or baking tray in the centre of the oven to heat up.

Roll out a portion of pizza dough on a clean floured benchtop to your desired pizza size, then place on a clean, dry baking tray dusted with a good amount of semolina or flour to prevent the pizza sticking.

Spread the sauce over the base and sprinkle with the garlic, then lightly with the parmesan. Arrange the tomato slices on top, then follow with the mozzarella. Brush the crust with a little olive oil, and season with salt and pepper.

Carefully transfer the pizza to the preheated pizza stone or baking tray, and replace in the centre of the oven. Cook until the pizza base is crispy – about 10–12 minutes with a pizza stone or 15–18 minutes on a tray.

Remove from the oven, top with the prosciutto, fresh basil leaves, and a drizzle of balsamic (if using) and olive oil. Season with pepper. The prosciutto is already salty, so taste before seasoning with salt.

Serves 4

Salmon, caper and cream cheese pizza

There's a great little Italian restaurant I often go to with my girlfriend, and for a while the salmon pizza is all we ate. I make my version of it at home now and it's still one of my favourites. Don't forget to give it a good squeeze of lemon before you eat it.

1 quantity pizza dough (see page 103 or use Turkish pizza bases)
¾ cup pizza sauce (see page 102)
handful freshly grated parmesan
½ cup cream cheese
10 smoked salmon pieces
3–4 tomatoes, topped and sliced
1 tbsp capers
salt and freshly cracked black pepper
few handfuls rocket
squeeze of lemon
extra virgin olive oil for drizzling

Preheat the oven to 220°C fan-bake (or as hot as your oven will go). Place your pizza stone or baking tray in the centre of the oven to heat up.

Roll out a portion of pizza dough on a clean floured benchtop to your desired pizza size, then place on a clean, dry baking tray dusted with a good amount of semolina or flour to prevent the pizza sticking.

Spread the sauce over the base and sprinkle with the parmesan. Add teaspoon-sized blobs of cream cheese all over the pizza, then scatter with the smoked salmon pieces. Arrange the tomato slices around the pizza, then sprinkle the capers over the top. Season with salt and pepper.

Carefully transfer the pizza to the preheated pizza stone or baking tray, and replace in the centre of the oven. Cook until the pizza base is crispy – about 10–12 minutes with a pizza stone, or 15–18 minutes on a tray.

Remove from the oven, arrange a little pile of rocket in the middle, then squeeze over a little lemon juice and drizzle with extra virgin olive oil.

Serves 4

Steak pizza with mustard cream

Mustard is a steak's best friend and they sure make a handsome pair on this pizza! Make sure you don't overcook the steak at the start; you just want to brown it quickly or it will be overcooked by the time you take it out of the oven.

1 tbsp hot English mustard
2 tsp mayonnaise
2 tsp cream
1 tsp lemon juice
olive oil for cooking
600g rump steak, trimmed
salt and freshly cracked black pepper
1 quantity pizza dough (see page 103 or use Turkish pizza bases)
¾ cup pizza sauce (see page 102)
2–3 cloves garlic, finely chopped
handful grated mozzarella
½ red onion, sliced
1 tsp chopped fresh thyme leaves
1 cup cherry tomatoes, halved, or 2–3 tomatoes, sliced
extra virgin olive oil for brushing

Preheat the oven to 220°C fan-bake (or as hot as your oven will go). Place your pizza stone or baking tray in the centre of the oven to heat up.

To make the mustard cream, mix the mustard, mayonnaise, cream and lemon juice in a small bowl. Set aside.

Heat a little olive oil in a frying pan over a high heat. Season the steak with salt and pepper, and sear for minute or so each side until browned. Remove from the pan and set aside to rest for 5 minutes. Once rested, cut into strips across the grain.

Roll out a portion of pizza dough on a clean floured benchtop to your desired pizza size, then place on a clean, dry baking tray dusted with a good amount of semolina or flour to prevent the pizza sticking.

Spread the sauce over the base and sprinkle with the garlic. Add some mozzarella, then top with the steak strips, sliced onion, thyme leaves and the tomatoes. Season with salt and pepper, and brush the crust with a little extra virgin olive oil.

Carefully transfer the pizza to the preheated pizza stone or baking tray, and replace in the centre of the oven. Cook until the pizza base is crispy – about 10–12 minutes with a pizza stone or 15–18 minutes on a tray.

Remove from the oven, drizzle with the mustard cream and serve.

Serves 4

Three cheese pizza

Sometimes all I feel like eating on my pizza is cheese. You can try using other combinations if you like . . . I find parmesan, mozzarella and blue to be delicious, however non-blue cheese fans might like to try Gruyere or Havarti, even goats cheese would be nice here.

1 quantity pizza dough (see page 103 or use Turkish pizza bases)
¾ cup pizza sauce (see page 102)
1–2 cloves garlic, finely chopped
1 large ball fresh mozzarella, sliced
handful freshly grated parmesan
½ cup crumbled creamy blue cheese
extra virgin olive oil for brushing
handful walnuts, roughly chopped
¼ cup fresh thyme leaves (and flowers if you have them)

Preheat the oven to 220°C fan-bake (or as hot as your oven will go). Place your pizza stone or baking tray in the centre of the oven to heat up.

Roll out a portion of pizza dough on a clean floured benchtop to your desired pizza size, then place on a clean, dry baking tray dusted with a good amount of semolina or flour to prevent the pizza sticking.

Spread the sauce over the base and sprinkle with the garlic. Cover with a few slices of mozzarella, then sprinkle with the parmesan and the crumbled blue cheese. Brush the crust with a little olive oil.

Carefully transfer the pizza to the preheated pizza stone or baking tray, and replace in the centre of the oven. Cook until the pizza base is crispy – about 10–12 minutes with a pizza stone or 15–18 minutes on a tray.

Remove from the oven and sprinkle with a few walnuts and some fresh thyme.

Chapter six

Mains

Serves 4

Easy butter chicken

I know that butter chicken is often sneered at for being 'western' and not a true Indian curry – but I think who cares if it tastes this good? Food for me isn't about strict rules, it's about enjoyment.

I got fed up with being constantly disappointed at being served second-rate butter chicken that didn't deliver on flavour, so I set about creating my own recipe that was easy to make at home. I think it needs to be served with hot, crispy naan bread, and I implore you to try making your own (see page 215) – but if you're short of time, bought will do just fine. If you like your curry spicy, add more chilli powder.

800g boneless, skinless chicken thighs, cut into bite-sized pieces
1 tbsp lemon juice
¼ cup plain unsweetened yoghurt
2 tsp paprika
2 tbsp neutral oil (rice bran or canola)
50g butter
2 cloves garlic, finely chopped
1 tsp finely chopped fresh ginger
2 tsp garam masala
1 tsp ground cardamom
1 tsp ground cinnamon
¼ tsp chilli powder
1 x 400g can tomato purée
1 tbsp brown sugar
½ cup chicken stock
½ cup cream
¼ cup plain unsweetened yoghurt
1 tsp dried fenugreek leaves (optional)
salt
chopped fresh parsley leaves to serve

Mix the chicken with the lemon juice, yoghurt and paprika in a bowl, cover and marinate in the fridge for 20 minutes.

Heat the oil in a frying pan over a high heat and sear the chicken pieces in batches until golden. Set aside.

Reduce the heat to medium-high, then add the butter, garlic, ginger, garam masala, cardamom, cinnamon and chilli. Cook, stirring constantly, for a few minutes until fragrant. Add the chicken pieces and the juices back to the pan. Add the tomato purée, sugar and chicken stock to the pan. Simmer gently for 15 minutes until reduced and the chicken is cooked through. Add the cream, yoghurt and fenugreek leaves if using, and simmer for another 5 minutes. Taste and season with salt, and sprinkle with the parsley.

Serve with basmati rice and naan bread (see page 215).

Serves 3–4

Chicken cacciatore

I used to work in an Italian restaurant in my late teens, and the chicken cacciatore was my favourite thing on the menu. It's healthy, packed full of flavour and can either be beefed up with new potatoes or pasta, and seasonal veges or a fresh salad with a few slices of ciabatta for a lighter meal. I've created this recipe as close to how the original tasted as I can remember (I think it's better!), and a few of my recipe testers scored it 9 out of 10 – so it's quite delicious. If you prefer to use chicken thighs or drumsticks, it'll work fine.

1 tbsp olive oil
4–5 chicken breasts (I leave the skin on)
1 large onion, finely chopped
4 cloves garlic, finely chopped
1 tbsp tomato paste
1 x 400g can chopped tomatoes
1 cup salt-reduced chicken stock
½ cup kalamata olives, pitted
2 tbsp capers
6 sundried tomatoes, roughly chopped
1 chargrilled red capsicum, sliced into strips (see page 214 or use storebought)
1 tbsp chopped rosemary leaves
large pinch chilli flakes
2 tsp brown sugar
1 tsp white wine vinegar

Preheat the oven to 220°C.

Heat the oil in a large frying pan over a medium-high heat, and brown the chicken breasts for 3–4 minutes on each side until golden brown. Remove from the pan and set aside.

Reduce the heat to medium, add the onion and garlic, and cook for 5 minutes until the onion is soft. Add the tomato paste and cook, stirring, for another few minutes. Add the tomatoes and chicken stock, and bring to the boil. Reduce to a simmer, add the chicken breasts back to the pan, along with the olives, capers, sundried tomato, capsicum, rosemary, chilli flakes, sugar and vinegar, and simmer very gently until the sauce has reduced and the chicken has cooked through. At this point, I like to place the pan (if it's ovenproof) in the oven for 5 minutes or so to brown up the top.

Serves 4

Mediterranean sausage bake

Sausages are a tasty classic Kiwi favourite. And while I'm a huge fan of bangers and mash and a good old sausage sizzle with onions, tomato sauce and white bread, there's no reason you can't use the humble sausage in a more sophisticated dish. It's all about using good-quality, fresh ingredients and the right flavour bases. The cannellini beans have a lovely texture and a nut-like flavour – and they make a nice change from potatoes.

1 tbsp olive oil
9 beef sausages
1 onion, finely chopped
4 cloves garlic, roughly chopped
1 x 420g can cannellini beans, rinsed
2 x 400g cans chopped tomatoes
½ cup kalamata olives
⅓ cup fresh oregano leaves, roughly chopped
1 tbsp chopped fresh thyme leaves
zest of 1 lemon
pinch chilli flakes (optional)
½ tsp salt
freshly cracked black pepper
2cm thick slice feta, crumbled
½ cup chopped fresh parsley leaves

Preheat the oven to 180°C.

Heat the olive oil in a saucepan over a high heat. Prick the sausages all over and fry them in the pan until golden brown all over. Prick again while in the pan if you need to. Drain on paper towels.

Place the sausages, onion, garlic, cannellini beans, tomatoes, olives, oregano, thyme, lemon zest, chilli flakes if using, and salt in a large oven dish. Finish with a good grind of pepper. Place in the oven and cook for 1 hour.

Taste and season with salt and pepper if needed, then top with the crumbled feta and fresh parsley.

Serves 4

Chicken Caesar salad with basil dressing

I've had some dreadful Caesar salads in my time and I'm sure you have too – overly rich, heavily salted, made with poor-quality ingredients and manufactured dressing. Done well, however, this salad can be a real delight. I think the magic lies in the dressing; it makes such a big difference using one that is good-quality and homemade. The leftover dressing can keep for up to a week in the fridge and is wonderful in sammies or wraps, with potato salad or as a dip. If you were pressed for time, you could just use a cooked chook and simply scatter chunks of it on the salad.

Dressing

1 free-range egg yolk
1 whole free-range egg
2 tsp lemon juice
1 tsp sugar
1 clove garlic, roughly chopped
150ml oil (canola or rice bran)
1 tbsp mayonnaise
5 anchovy fillets
½ cup chopped fresh basil leaves
salt and freshly cracked black pepper

Salad

3 tbsp olive oil
3–4 chicken breasts, skin on
½ loaf ciabatta, crusts removed and cut into 3–4cm cubes
1 cup bacon, chopped into large pieces
2 cos lettuces
½ telegraph cucumber, halved lengthways, cored and shaved into slices with a peeler
2–3 free-range eggs, poached or hard-boiled

Preheat the oven to 220°C.

To make the dressing, whizz the egg yolk, egg, lemon juice, sugar and garlic in a food processor until well combined and pale, about 1 minute. With the motor running, add the oil very slowly in a thin stream until it is all used up. The dressing will thicken. Add the mayonnaise, anchovies and basil, and process until well incorporated and smooth. Taste and season with salt and pepper. Add more lemon juice or sugar if you like. Keep covered in the fridge until you need it.

Heat a large frying pan with 1 tablespoon of olive oil over a high heat. Season the chicken with salt and pepper, and cook, skin side down, for 3 minutes or until the skin is golden and crispy. Turn over and cook for another 2 minutes. Transfer the chicken to a baking dish and bake, uncovered, in the oven for 15 minutes. Remove and rest in the baking dish for 15 minutes.

While the chicken is resting, coat the ciabatta cubes in the remaining olive oil and season with salt. Bake in the oven for 5–10 minutes or until golden on the outside and still a little soft inside.

Cook the bacon pieces until crispy in the same pan you cooked the chicken in. Remove and drain on paper towels.

To serve, toss the lettuce leaves with 1 tablespoon of the dressing. Arrange the lettuce and cucumber on a serving platter or bowl. Slice the chicken breasts and arrange on top. Place the eggs and bacon on top, then sprinkle the salad with the croutons. Drizzle with extra dressing and serve.

Serves 4

Crispy fish wraps with mango salsa

This recipe is a tasty and ingenious way to use some of the less expensive types of fish such as hoki, although you can use whatever fish you like. The punchy Mexican flavours are fantastic, the salsa is fresh and clean, and the corn-chip crumb adds a salty crunch – a huge hit with the kids! Assembling wraps like this is a fun hands-on way for the family to eat a meal, too.

1 cup plain salted corn chips, crushed into a coarse crumb
1 cup breadcrumbs
2–3 tbsp plain flour
1 free-range egg, lightly beaten
600–700g firm white fish fillets
salt and freshly cracked black pepper
2 tsp sweet paprika

Salsa
½ red onion, finely diced
1 clove garlic, finely chopped
¾ cup fresh or canned mango, thinly sliced
1 avocado, finely diced
4–5 ripe tomatoes, cored, deseeded and diced
½ cup fresh coriander leaves, roughly chopped
1 red chilli, deseeded and chopped (optional)
lime juice to taste
sugar to taste

To cook and assemble
8–10 flour tortillas
2 tbsp neutral oil for cooking (rice bran or canola)
1 cup grated cheese
chopped iceberg lettuce
sour cream
extra fresh coriander leaves
lime wedges

Preheat the oven to 180°C.

Mix the corn-chip crumbs with the breadcrumbs in a bowl. Place the flour in a separate bowl and the beaten egg in another.

Season the fish fillets with salt and pepper, then sprinkle with the paprika. Dust lightly with flour, then dip each fillet in the beaten egg, then the crumbs. Cover and put in the fridge while you prep the rest of the ingredients.

To make the salsa, mix the red onion, garlic, mango, avocado, tomatoes, coriander and chilli if using, in a bowl. Add the lime juice and sugar. Taste and season with salt and pepper. Set aside.

Wrap the tortillas in foil and heat in the oven for 5–10 minutes.

Heat the oil in a frying pan over a medium-high heat. Cook the fish fillets in batches for a few minutes on each side until the coating is golden and crispy and the fish is only just cooked through. Drain on paper towels.

I like to serve everything on the table in separate dishes so people can make up their own tortillas.

Serves 4–6

Creamy chicken and vegetable pie

This is one of my signature dishes, and perhaps my all-time favourite thing to cook and to serve. I also suspect this is how I won my husband Mike over for good, so it deserves its spot on the cover! I've played with many recipe variations over the years and this one is getting pretty darn close to perfect. Try it, and I dare say it may become an instant family favourite.

800g boneless, skinless chicken thighs
2 tbsp olive oil
salt and freshly cracked black pepper
¾ cup chopped bacon
5 cloves garlic, finely chopped
1 leek, white part only, sliced
2 carrots, chopped into 1cm dice (any larger and they won't cook through)
1 tsp chopped fresh thyme leaves
250g brown button mushrooms, sliced
1½ cups chopped spinach, washed and excess moisture squeezed out
75g butter
½ cup plain flour
1½ cups milk
⅓ cup cream
⅓ cup freshly grated parmesan
2 tsp wholegrain mustard
2–3 sheets flaky puff pastry
¼ cup milk
1 free-range egg

Preheat the oven to 180°C fan-bake.

Coat the chicken pieces in 1 tablespoon of the olive oil, and season with salt and pepper. Place in a baking dish and bake in the oven for 15–20 minutes until golden and cooked through. Cool, then shred into bite-sized pieces.

Grease a pie dish.

While the chicken is cooking, fry the bacon until crispy, then drain on paper towels.

Wipe out the pan and heat the remaining olive oil over a medium heat. Add the garlic, leek, carrot and thyme, and cook for 5 minutes. Add the mushrooms and spinach, and cook for another 5 minutes until the excess liquid from the mushrooms has evaporated. Return the chicken pieces and bacon to the pan, mix to combine and turn off the heat.

To make the sauce, heat the butter in a saucepan over a medium heat. Stir in the flour and cook for 4 minutes until the flour is cooked out (do not brown). Remove from the heat and slowly pour in the milk, whisking continuously to avoid lumps forming. Whisk in the cream and parmesan and return the pan to the heat. Cook, stirring, for about 5 minutes or until the sauce has thickened. Stir in the mustard. Taste and season with salt and pepper. Add the sauce to the chicken mixture and mix gently to combine.

Line the prepared pie dish with the pastry. Spoon in the filling and top with a lid of pastry. Seal the edges with a little milk and crimp the edges with your fingers. Make a funny shape from the pastry scraps and place on top. Lightly beat the egg and remaining milk together, and brush over the pastry. Cut a couple of air holes. Bake in the oven for 40 minutes or until the pastry is cooked through and golden.

Serves 4

Prawn fajitas

I adore Mexican-style food. I wish people knew how easy it was to create delicious, healthy Mexican meals at home without expensive kits. It's a case of using key base flavours and going wild with garnishes and condiments! I get a bit out of control with accompaniments sometimes, because I love my table covered with little bowls of tasty sauces and bits and bobs of different textures and flavours. You can easily use chicken instead of the prawns for a more cost-effective option, too.

Salsa

1 corn cob, barbecued and kernels removed
1 tomato, cored, deseeded and diced
⅓ cucumber, cut in half lengthways, deseeded and diced
½ red onion, diced
1 tsp lime juice
2 tbsp chopped fresh coriander
salt and freshly cracked black pepper

Fajitas

6–10 flour tortillas
1 tbsp oil (rice bran or canola)
1 onion, sliced
2 cloves garlic, roughly chopped
1–2 chargrilled red capsicums (see page 214)
1 red chilli, deseeded and chopped (optional)
1 tsp smoked paprika
1½ tsp sweet paprika
½ tsp ground cumin
½ tsp sugar
⅓ cup water
600g prawns, shelled, deveined and tails removed
juice of 1 lime

To assemble

150g sour cream
¼ cup chopped fresh coriander leaves
guacamole (see page 211)
lettuce leaves
lime wedges

Combine all the salsa ingredients in a bowl, cover and refrigerate.

Preheat the oven to 180°C.

Wrap the tortillas in foil and put them in the oven for about 10 minutes until heated through.

Heat the oil in a frying pan over a medium heat. Add the onion, garlic, capsicums, chilli (if using), the paprikas, cumin and sugar, and stir-fry for a few more minutes until the onion is soft. Turn up the heat, add the water and simmer for a few minutes. Add the prawns and cook on high for a few more minutes until the prawns are only just cooked through. Remove from the heat and squeeze the lime juice over. Taste and season.

Combine the sour cream with the chopped coriander.

Serve all the components on the table in nice serving dishes, so everyone can make their own fajitas.

Serves 4

Prosciutto-wrapped chicken with creamy white wine sauce

This really is a cracker of a dish, especially if you're looking to wow your diners. Visually it's impressive, and the combination of tender chicken, salty crispy prosciutto and smooth creamy sauce is lip-smackingly good. In winter, I serve it on a bed of fresh green veges such as leeks and beans. In summer, or for a lighter meal, you could swap the veges for a green salad. The crispy bread is great for mopping up the delicious sauce. If you're on a budget, you can use streaky bacon instead of prosciutto.

200g ricotta cheese
zest of 1 large lemon
½ cup freshly grated parmesan
½ cup fresh basil leaves
2 tbsp chopped fresh parsley leaves
freshly cracked black pepper
8 boneless, skinless chicken thighs
8 slices prosciutto
2 tbsp olive oil
1 tbsp butter
1 shallot, finely chopped
2 cloves garlic, finely chopped
½ cup white wine
½ cup salt-reduced chicken stock
½ cup cream
1 tbsp chopped fresh chives

Preheat the oven to 180°C.

Mix the ricotta, lemon zest, parmesan, basil and half the chopped parsley in a bowl. Season with pepper.

Open out a chicken thigh and place between two sheets of cling film. Place on a chopping board or clean benchtop and pound with a meat mallet or rolling pin to flatten to an even thickness of 1–2cm. Repeat with the rest of the thighs.

Lay a strip of prosciutto on a clean chopping board. Top with a chicken thigh. Spread a tablespoon of the ricotta mixture over the thigh. Carefully roll up the whole chicken parcel from the long end, and gently place in a metal roasting pan. Repeat with the remaining chicken and prosciutto. Brush the chicken parcels with 1 tablespoon of the olive oil, and season with pepper. (Don't add salt at this point, as the prosciutto is already salty.)

Bake in the oven for 35 minutes.

Remove the chicken from the pan, cover and keep warm. Return the pan to the stovetop over a medium heat. Add the butter, shallot and garlic, and cook for a few minutes to soften. Add the white wine and chicken stock, and simmer until reduced by half. Add the cream and simmer until the sauce is thick enough to coat the back of a spoon. Add the remaining parsley and the chives. Taste and season with pepper.

To serve, arrange the chicken on a serving plate, then spoon over the sauce. Serve with warmed crusty bread, salad and new potatoes.

Serves 4–6

Tender slow-roasted chicken with crispy potatoes

This is not just your average roast chook. Slow-roasting a chicken like this and then letting it rest for a good amount of time delivers incredible results. Say goodbye to dry chicken... the meat you carve up using this recipe will be succulent and moist, and full of flavour. Slow-roasting might not be ideal for a weeknight, but it's definitely worth trying this out for your next Sunday roast.

Chicken

1 size 20 whole chicken
stuffing (see page 214)
1 sprig fresh rosemary
60g butter
1 tbsp olive oil
½ tsp salt
black pepper
¾ cup chicken stock
1 onion, chopped
3 whole cloves garlic

Potatoes

5–6 roasting potatoes, peeled and cut into even-sized pieces
1 tbsp olive oil

Gravy

2–3 tbsp plain flour mixed with ½ cup water
1 chicken stock cube mixed with the flour and water mixture

green vegetables to serve

Preheat the oven to 120°C.

Remove the chicken from its packaging and place in a roasting dish. Pat the whole bird dry with paper towels. Ensure there are no packaging pads left in the cavity. Pack the cavity with the stuffing. Thread a soaked skewer or a stick of rosemary through the skin like a needle, to hold the cavity closed.

Very carefully, using your finger, separate the skin from the left breast meat as far down as you can. Be very careful not to rip the skin. Repeat with the right breast. Cut the butter into thin, wide slices and slide under the breast skin, an even amount on each side. Drizzle the oil over the chicken and rub to coat evenly. Sprinkle the salt over, then crack some pepper on top. Pour the chicken stock into the roasting tray with the chicken, and add the onion and garlic. Bake in the lower part of the oven for 3 hours, basting the chicken every half hour or so.

With half an hour to go, boil the potatoes in a saucepan of salted water until about half done. Drain, and place the potatoes back in the pan. Return to the heat for 10 seconds to dry out the excess moisture. Add the olive oil and a good amount of salt, then shake the pot with the lid on, to rough up the outside of the potatoes a little. Place in a baking dish, making sure each potato has plenty of space around it (this is important for crispy potatoes).

Remove the chicken from the oven. Place on a plate, cover and set aside to rest for 15 minutes.

Turn the oven up to 220°C fan-bake, and put the potatoes in to crisp up while the chicken rests. Don't be tempted to turn

Recipe continued over page

them over – just leave as they are until cooked.

To make the gravy, skim most of the fat off the surface of the chicken roasting juices (the garlic and onion should be almost liquefied). Place the whole roasting tray over a medium heat, and mix in the water, flour and stock cube. Scrape all the bits off the bottom with a wooden spoon. Continue to stir as the gravy thickens, cooking for 7–10 minutes. Add more flour or water depending on how thick you like your gravy. Taste and season with salt and pepper. When thickened, strain and pour into a gravy jug. Serve with your favourite veges and smother the roast potatoes in gravy.

Serves 4

Thai chicken satay skewers

There can't be many people out there who aren't partial to the odd Thai chicken satay skewer (or 10). Unsurprisingly, this has become a staple in our house, whether I serve them as nibbles or in a huge pile on a platter to devour for dinner with steamed rice. You can leave the lemongrass out if you must, but I would recommend getting a few stalks from your local fruit shop next time you're there and keeping them in the freezer.

Chicken

1 onion, chopped
3 cloves garlic, chopped
2 tsp finely grated fresh ginger
1 tsp ground coriander
1 tsp ground cumin
½ tsp ground turmeric
3 tbsp fish sauce
2 tbsp brown sugar
zest and juice of 1 lime
1 lemongrass stalk, finely chopped or 3 tsp lemongrass paste
2 tbsp vegetable oil (I use peanut)
8–10 skinless, boneless chicken thighs, cut into pieces

Sauce

1 cup roasted peanuts, finely chopped
½ cup coconut cream
2 tsp sesame oil
2 cloves garlic, finely chopped
1 tbsp soy sauce
1 tbsp brown sugar
1 tbsp fish sauce
1 tbsp fresh lime juice

vegetable oil for cooking
fresh coriander leaves to serve
lime wedges to serve

To make the marinade, blend all the ingredients except the chicken pieces in a food processor until you have a smooth paste. Or just chop everything very finely and mix by hand. Place in a bowl with the chicken pieces and coat well. Cover and marinate in the fridge for at least 20 minutes. Put several wooden skewers to soak in cold water.

To make the sauce, combine all the ingredients in a saucepan and bring to a gentle simmer. Simmer for 5 minutes. Taste and, if need be, add more brown sugar, fish sauce or lime juice until the balance of flavours is to your liking.

Thread the chicken onto the skewers. Heat some oil in a hot frying or grill pan, or on a barbecue heated to high, and cook the skewers until the chicken is cooked through.

Arrange the skewers on a plate and either drizzle the sauce over the chicken or serve it in a dipping bowl on the side. Serve with coriander leaves and lime wedges.

Serves 4

Scallops with cauliflower purée and lemon and thyme oil

I created this dish as an entrée for a dinner party, and it was so successful that it's become one of my favourite go-to recipes for entertaining. It's simple to make but it looks great and the textures are fantastic. Be careful when cooking the scallops – they only need a brief whisk around the hot pan to caramelise the outside. If you overcook them, they will go rubbery. To save cooking time, the prosciutto, thyme oil and purée can be done in advance, so you just cook the scallops when you're ready.

2 slices prosciutto, halved

Purée

4 heaped cups chopped cauliflower, cut into small pieces (about 1 medium-sized cauliflower)
50g butter
½ cup cream
salt and white pepper

Lemon and thyme oil

2 heaped tbsp chopped fresh thyme leaves
½ cup neutral oil (rice bran or canola)
zest of 1 lemon

1–2 tbsp butter
20 scallops
squeeze of lemon
microherbs to serve

Preheat the oven to 160°C.

Place the prosciutto slices on a baking tray lined with baking paper and bake in the oven for 10 minutes or until crisp. Set aside.

Place the cauliflower pieces, butter and cream in a saucepan, cover and simmer for about 15 minutes until tender. Purée in a food processor or with a stick blender until silky smooth. You can pass it through a sieve if you like. Taste and season with salt and white pepper. Set aside and keep warm.

To make the thyme oil, bash the thyme leaves in a mortar and pestle to release the flavours. (Or chop then rub with your fingers.) Place the oil, lemon zest and thyme in a small saucepan and heat gently over a medium-low heat for 5 minutes (being careful not to boil or simmer). Pour into a small jug ready for serving.

Heat the butter in a frying pan over a high heat. Season the scallops lightly with salt and pepper. Add the scallops to the pan and cook for a minute or so, turning after about 40 seconds, then cook on the other side for 10 seconds (only one side needs to be caramelised). Season lightly with salt and pepper and squeeze a little lemon over.

To serve, spoon the cauliflower purée in the middle of four serving plates. Top with four or five scallops each, caramelised side up. Drizzle the lemon and thyme oil over the plate. Top with a piece of prosciutto, sprinkle with microherbs and serve.

Serves 4–6

Coq au vin

This is my version of the much-loved classic French dish. Legend has it that *coq au vin* (literally French for 'rooster in wine') has been around since the time of ancient Gaul and Julius Caesar, although the actual recipe wasn't written down until the early twentieth century. If a recipe has survived for that long, there must be a very good reason for it – it's delicious, soulful food. Long may it live on in my cookbook, too. Serve with steamed new potatoes or pasta, and seasonal veges.

1 tbsp olive oil
300g shoulder bacon, chopped into large chunks, or use lardons
1 size 24 whole chicken, quartered or 1.5kg chicken pieces, skin on
½ cup brandy or cognac
7–9 small brown onions, peeled
8 cloves garlic, peeled
250g brown button mushrooms
2 sprigs rosemary
1 tsp fennel seeds
handful fresh thyme leaves
2 bay leaves
750ml red wine (Beaujolais or pinot noir)
1 cup salt-reduced chicken stock
freshly cracked black pepper
¼ cup plain flour
50g butter
salt and white pepper
½ cup chopped fresh parsley leaves

Preheat the oven to 180°C.

Heat the oil in a large frying pan (ovenproof if possible) over a high heat and fry the bacon until coloured and cooked through. Remove and set aside. Add the chicken pieces to the pan and cook them, skin side down, in the bacon fat until golden brown, 5–6 minutes. Drain the excess fat from the pan.

Add the brandy or cognac and flambé until the flames disappear; be careful not to get too close as the flames can be quite ferocious. Turn the heat up and add the onions, garlic, bacon, mushrooms, herbs, wine and chicken stock. Season with pepper.

Cover and place in the oven for 2 hours. If you don't have an ovenproof frying pan, transfer everything to a covered casserole dish at this point. After 2 hours, carefully remove the chicken pieces and keep warm.

Return the pan to the stovetop or tip the sauce back into a frying pan if using a casserole, and simmer to reduce the liquid by about a third. Add the flour and butter, whisking to combine, then cook until the sauce is thick enough to coat the back of a spoon. Taste and season with salt and white pepper.

Pour the sauce over the chicken, then top with the chopped fresh parsley.

Serves 4–6

Smoked fish pie

There's nothing quite as comforting or delicious to me as a good smoked fish pie.

1¼ cups milk
1 cup cream
2 whole cloves
1 bay leaf
75g butter
1 onion, finely chopped
2 cloves garlic, finely chopped
2 carrots, cut into 1cm dice
3 stalks celery, finely chopped
1 red capsicum, cut into 1cm dice
1 leek, white part only, roughly chopped
¼ cup plain flour
½ cup white wine
600g good-quality smoked fish, bones and scales removed, broken up into large chunks
1 cup finely chopped spinach
2 tbsp capers, rinsed
2 gherkins, chopped (optional)
1 tbsp lemon zest
¼ cup chopped fresh flat-leaf parsley leaves
1 tbsp chopped fresh dill
¼ cup cream
salt and white pepper
7 agria potatoes, peeled and roughly chopped
25g butter
freshly ground black pepper
3 soft-boiled free-range eggs, quartered
½ cup finely grated parmesan

Preheat the oven to 180°C.

To make the filling, place the milk, cream, cloves and bay leaf in a saucepan and place over a medium heat. Bring to a simmer and gently simmer for 5 minutes, then strain. Set aside.

In a separate saucepan, melt the butter over a medium heat. Add the onion and garlic, and cook gently until soft. Add the carrot, celery, capsicum and leek, and cook for about 10 minutes. Stir the flour in thoroughly. Cook out the flour for 4 minutes, stirring regularly.

Slowly pour the warm milk mixture into the vegetable mixture, whisking continuously to avoid lumps forming. Add the wine and allow to gently simmer for 10 minutes. Be careful not to burn the filling.

Gently fold the smoked fish, spinach, capers, gherkin, lemon zest, parsley, dill and cream into the filling mixture. Taste and season with salt and white pepper. Set aside.

Place the potatoes in a saucepan of salted water and bring to the boil. Cook until tender. Drain, then place the potatoes back in the pan. Return to a low heat for a minute or so to dry out the excess moisture. Mash or pass through a potato ricer. Beat in the butter. Taste and season with salt and black pepper. If you like a chunkier texture, just mash the potatoes roughly.

Spoon the filling into a large pie dish. Press the eggs into the mixture. Top with a generous amount of mash, then sprinkle the parmesan over.

Bake in the oven for 20–30 minutes or until the topping is golden and crisp.

Sprinkle with a little more chopped parsley and serve with a green salad.

Serves 6

Slow-roasted pork shoulder with crackling and apple gravy

I think I might be one of the country's biggest roast fanatics. If I had to choose my favourite roast of all time, I think I'd be torn between this and my slow-roasted chicken (page 136). It generally depends on what's on special that week! You'll have to give them both a go and let me know what you think. Cooking the pork slowly with the bone in like this results in juicy, tender meat that falls apart on your fork. And when it's slathered in rich apple gravy and served with crunchy salted crackling, it doesn't get much better.

1 x 2kg pork shoulder, bone in
¼ cup extra virgin olive oil
salt
1 tbsp fennel seeds
2 tsp cumin seeds
1½ cups chicken stock
½ cup pinot gris
1 stick rosemary
4 cloves garlic, peeled
1 onion, peeled and roughly chopped
1 Granny Smith apple, peeled, cored and sliced
¼ cup flour mixed into a paste with a little water
cracked black pepper

Remove the pork from the fridge 30 minutes before cooking to allow it to come to room temperature.

Preheat the oven to 220°C fan-bake. Pat the pork dry with paper towels. If not already done, carefully score through the fat with a small sharp knife in lines 1cm apart. Be careful not to go too deep and pierce the skin. Place in a metal roasting dish (preferably with a lid). Drizzle with the olive oil. Rub a good amount of salt and the cumin and fennel seeds into the skin, pushing them into the cuts as well.

Cook uncovered in the oven for 30 minutes – the crackling should start popping and puffing. Turn the heat down to 140°C (non fan-bake). Pour the chicken stock and white wine into the bottom of the roasting dish. Add the stick of rosemary, garlic, onion and one of the sliced apples. Cover with either the lid of the roasting dish or 2 layers of tinfoil. Cook for another 3½ hours, basting the sides of the meat every 30 minutes or so (do not baste the crackling).

Remove the pork from the roasting dish to a plate. Remove the crackling in one piece with a knife, and set aside on a piece of foil, skin side up. Cover the meat with tinfoil, rest for at least 10 minutes, and keep warm until ready to carve.

Turn the oven to grill at 200°C. Sprinkle the crackling with a little more salt and put it back in the oven, skin side up, near

Recipe continued over page

the top (turn up the edges of the foil so the fat doesn't drip out). Cook until the crackling is browned and crispy. Drain on paper towels.

To make the gravy, skim some of the fat off the top of the lovely liquefied apple and onion cooking liquid. Place the roasting dish on the stove over a medium heat. Cook to reduce by a third. Add the flour mixture and whisk, cooking until thickened, making sure you scrape up any of the stuck-on bits. Taste and season with salt and pepper. Strain through a sieve and reserve in a jug.

Carve the meat and serve with roasted potatoes (see page 136) and seasonal veges.

Serves 4

Snapper with butternut purée and orange butter sauce

This recipe is a nice way to turn a simple piece of fish into an elegant meal.

Butternut purée
1 butternut pumpkin
50g butter, plus extra for cooking
salt and freshly cracked black pepper

Orange butter sauce
1 cup white wine
25g butter
¼ cup orange juice

1 tbsp butter
1 cup snowpeas, topped
1 spring onion, finely chopped
4–5 large snapper or terakihi fillets

Pop the butternut in the microwave for 1 minute on high to soften. Peel and core the butternut, then cut into small even-sized pieces.

Heat the butter in a large frying pan over a medium heat. Add the butternut and cook, stirring occasionally, for 30–40 minutes or until it is cooked through.

Process to a purée in a blender or mash with a masher. Taste and season with salt and pepper. Keep warm.

In a small saucepan, simmer the wine until reduced by two-thirds. Add the butter and orange juice and whisk well to combine. Taste and season with salt and pepper. Keep warm until ready to serve.

Heat the butter in a pan over a medium-high heat. Add the snowpeas and spring onion and sauté until tender.

Season the fish fillets with salt and pepper.

Heat a little butter in a frying pan over a high heat. Pan-fry the fish until just underdone (it will keep cooking).

To serve, spoon the purée onto four plates. Top with the fish, then a drizzle of the sauce. Serve with the sautéed vegetables.

Serves 2–3

Salmon and cabbage red curry

I created this recipe one day when I had a lone salmon fillet in the fridge. I didn't feel like pan-frying it, so I made a quick Thai curry for lunch instead. It was a winner – easy to make and so incredibly delicious that I just had to include it in my book. Although salmon is a rich fish, the lime juice and the fresh Southeast Asian flavours cut through it nicely. You could also use green or yellow curry paste, and white fish and prawns will also work just as well.

½ onion
2 cloves garlic
1 tsp grated fresh ginger
1 red chilli (optional)
2 tbsp Thai red curry paste
zest of 1 lime
1 cup coconut milk
1 tbsp oil (peanut if you have it, or canola)
1 cup chicken stock
½ green or Savoy cabbage, finely chopped
500–600g salmon, skin and bones removed, cut into chunky pieces
1 tbsp brown sugar
1 tbsp fish sauce
1 tbsp lime juice
¼ cup chopped fresh coriander leaves and stalks
½ cup roasted peanuts, chopped

Process the onion, garlic, ginger, chilli if using, curry paste and lime zest in a food processor or pound in a mortar and pestle until it forms a smooth paste. Add a little coconut milk to bring it together if necessary.

Heat the oil in a frying pan over a medium heat, add the paste and stir-fry for about 5 minutes until aromatic. Add the remaining coconut milk and chicken stock, and continue to simmer for about 5 minutes. Add the cabbage and simmer until nearly cooked through but still al dente. Add the salmon pieces and cook until the salmon is still slightly underdone. Add the sugar, fish sauce and lime juice, stir gently and add more of each until the balance of hot, salty, sweet and sour flavours is to your liking. Stir through half the coriander.

Serve with steamed rice (I use brown rice), and garnish with the peanuts and remaining coriander.

Serves 2–3

Creamy spinach and salmon pasta

Everyone I make this dish for raves about it, and it's not hard to see why. Delicate fresh salmon pieces cooked to perfection and bound in a light cream sauce with spinach and hot, fresh ribbons of pasta. It's quick and easy to make (another one-dish wonder) and it's guaranteed to impress anyone you serve it to – whether it be a hungry family on a weeknight or fancy dinner guests. I hope you enjoy it.

1½ cups chopped spinach or baby spinach leaves
1 x 400g packet fresh fettuccine
2 tbsp butter
3 large cloves garlic, chopped
1 tbsp plain flour
½ cup good-quality white wine
1 cup cream
zest of 1 lemon
500g salmon fillet, skinned and boned, chopped into bite-sized pieces
½ cup freshly grated parmesan
salt and freshly cracked black pepper
1 tbsp chopped fresh dill
5–6 fresh basil leaves, chopped roughly
chopped fresh parsley leaves to garnish
extra parmesan to garnish
lemon cheeks or wedges to serve

Blanch the spinach in boiling water, then refresh in cold water. Squeeze out the excess moisture and set aside.

Bring a saucepan of salted water to the boil and cook the pasta according to the packet instructions. Drain and set aside until needed.

Melt the butter in a frying pan over a medium heat and sauté the garlic for 3–4 minutes. Add the flour and cook for another 4–5 minutes. Add the wine slowly, whisking while you add it to avoid lumps forming. Add the cream, lemon zest, salmon, blanched spinach and parmesan. Simmer for 5 minutes until the sauce has thickened and the salmon is cooked through. Taste and season with salt and pepper.

Stir through the dill and basil. Toss through the cooked pasta and garnish with parsley, extra parmesan and lemon cheeks.

Serves 4–6

Slow-cooked steak, Guinness and cheese pie

I am a great lover of pies, and have eaten far too many to mention in my time (both homemade and, yes, the nasty bought variety). This is a delicious way to use a cheaper cut of beef and turn it into a dish you'd be happy to be served up in any bistro. You can use a slow cooker set to low instead of the oven – just add more liquid to ensure it doesn't dry out. You can also make the filling in advance and keep it in the fridge until you need it.

2kg stewing steak, cut into chunks
4 tbsp plain flour
2 tbsp olive oil
1 onion, chopped
4 cloves garlic, finely chopped
2 tbsp tomato paste
3 tsp brown sugar
1 tsp mustard powder
1 x 330ml can Guinness or other dark ale
1½ cups beef jus or stock (I use Essential Cuisine)
250g button mushrooms, chopped
1 whole carrot
1 stalk celery, including leaves
1 bay leaf
salt and freshly cracked black pepper
3 sheets flaky puff pastry
200g sliced cheddar cheese
1 free-range egg, lightly beaten
¼ cup milk

Preheat the oven to 140°C.

Dust the beef pieces in flour.

Heat 1 tablespoon of olive oil over a high heat in a large deep ovenproof frying pan. If you don't have an ovenproof pan, just transfer everything to a casserole dish before cooking it in the oven. Brown the beef all over in batches. You may need to add a little more oil for each batch. Set aside.

Add the remaining olive oil to the pan and sauté the onion, garlic, tomato paste, sugar and mustard for 5 minutes. Add the beer and jus to the pan and simmer for a few minutes. Then add the mushrooms, carrot, celery and bay leaf.

Add the beef back to the pan, cover and cook in the oven for 3 hours. Remove from the oven, taste and season with salt and pepper. Leave the filling to cool slightly, then remove the carrot and celery.

Increase the oven temperature to 180°C. Grease a large casserole or pie dish.

Line the prepared dish with the pastry. Prick the bottom of the pastry with a fork a few times. Spoon in the beef filling, then layer the cheese slices on top. Top with another sheet of pastry, and seal and crimp the edges. Lightly beat the egg and remaining milk together, and brush over the pastry. Cut a couple of air holes in the pastry top. (Here you can cut a funny pastry shape if you are so inclined.)

Cook in the oven for about 30 minutes or until the pastry is cooked and golden brown. Serve with tomato sauce and salad.

Serves 2

Steak with creamy mushroom, bacon and garlic sauce

A big steak with creamy garlicky mushroom sauce is usually a hot favourite for the lads (and some ladies, like me). This one is so easy to make at home and doesn't take long either. The thing to remember is you really have to let that meat rest for 8–10 minutes so it retains its juices. Don't skip the step and ruin all your hard work! Serve this one up to the love of your life, with corn and a green salad for a summer meal, or potatoes and veges, and watch their face light up with delight.

olive oil for cooking
½ cup finely chopped bacon
1 shallot, finely chopped
3 cloves garlic, finely chopped
250g button mushrooms, sliced
½ cup salt-reduced chicken stock
1 tsp red or white wine vinegar
½ cup cream
1 tsp wholegrain mustard
1 tsp chopped fresh rosemary or thyme leaves
salt and freshly cracked black pepper
600g good-quality steak (I use scotch fillet)
chopped fresh parsley leaves to garnish

Heat 1 teaspoon of oil over a medium heat, add the bacon and fry until crispy. Drain the excess fat from the pan, reduce the heat to medium-low and add the shallot and garlic. Cook for a few minutes until soft. Add the mushrooms and cook for about 5 minutes. Add the chicken stock and vinegar, then let everything simmer away to reduce by half.

Add the cream, mustard and rosemary or thyme. Simmer for another 5 minutes or until the sauce is thick enough to coat the back of a spoon and is a nice consistency for pouring onto a steak. Taste and season with salt and a crack of pepper.

Season the steaks with salt and pepper. Heat a little oil in another frying pan over a high heat, then cook the steaks until medium-rare or to your liking. Cover with foil and rest for 5–10 minutes before serving. Tip the juices from the plate into the sauce, and mix to combine. Briefly reheat the sauce just before serving.

Serve the steak with the sauce spooned on top and the parsley sprinkled over.

Serves 2–3

Indian spiced steak with turmeric fried potatoes and spinach cream

This recipe is me throwing a bit of a Kiwi summer twist on a curry. You still get those lovely aromatic Indian flavours but as a lighter meal. The potatoes and steak are great done on the barbecue. I leave my potatoes unpeeled for this – as well as leaving more flavour and nutrients, I like the look of them. You could use chicken instead of steak for this one if that's more your thing.

600–800g steak (I use scotch fillet)
oil for frying

Marinade

2 tbsp neutral oil (rice bran or canola)
½ tsp cumin seeds
1 tsp lemon juice
½ tsp curry powder
½ tsp paprika
½ tsp turmeric
½ tsp ground coriander
1 large clove garlic, crushed
1 thumb-sized piece ginger, finely grated
¼ tsp ground chilli
good crack of pepper and a pinch of salt

6–8 agria potatoes, cut into large bite-sized chunks
1 tsp turmeric
salt and freshly ground pepper

200g spinach, washed
½ cup unsweetened yoghurt
1 clove garlic, finely chopped

Combine all the marinade ingredients in a bowl and mix well to combine. Either add the steaks to the bowl, mix well to coat and cover with cling film, or transfer the marinade and steak to a Ziploc bag. Refrigerate for at least 30 minutes.

Add the potatoes to a pot of cold salted water. Bring to the boil, then reduce to a simmer for 15 minutes until almost cooked through. Drain, then place the potatoes back in the pan. Return to the heat for a minute or so to dry out the excess moisture. Add the turmeric, season with salt and pepper and mix gently to combine, but try not to break up the potatoes too much.

To make the spinach sauce, blanch the spinach leaves in boiling water until tender. Drain, then add the yoghurt and garlic to the spinach, and purée or mash until smooth. Taste and season with salt and pepper.

Heat a pan or barbecue hotplate to medium-high heat. Add 1 tablespoon of oil and fry the potatoes until the outsides are golden brown.

Cook the steaks in a pan or on a barbecue grill over a high heat for a couple of minutes each side or until cooked to your liking. Remove from the heat and rest for 5 minutes.

Serve the steak over the potatoes and drizzle with the spinach sauce.

Serves 2

Duck breasts with tangy berry sauce

Duck breast isn't cooked very often in the average home kitchen, but I hope that changes soon because it's a beautiful rich meat that lends itself to a huge variety of flavours. Some people have a notion that duck is 'fatty', which makes me sad. Most of the fat is rendered out at the start here, and the crispy skin that's left is absolutely divine and should not be left on the side of the plate! Unlike chicken, duck can be eaten medium-rare, so don't panic when you see the pinkish flesh. If it's overcooked, it will go rubbery. This is a great dinner party meal and is delicious with sautéed cabbage and pumpkin mash.

2 duck breasts, skin on
salt
1 tbsp butter
2 shallots, finely chopped
¼ tsp ground ginger
½ tsp Chinese five-spice
½ cup red wine
1 cup chicken stock
2 tsp sugar
¼ tsp chilli powder
25g butter
1 cup fresh or frozen mixed berries or boysenberries
freshly cracked black pepper
2 tbsp finely chopped spring onions to garnish

Preheat the oven to 220°C fan-bake.

Pat the skin of the duck breasts dry with paper towels. With a sharp knife, very carefully score criss-cross lines in the skin, but be careful not to go too deep and pierce the flesh. Rub salt into the skin.

Place the breasts skin side down in a cold frying pan. Place over a medium-high heat for 6–7 minutes, or until the skin is golden brown and crispy and most of the fat has been rendered out. Remove the breasts from the pan and place skin side up in a roasting tray. (Keep the fat – it makes amazing roasted potatoes!) Bake the duck in the oven for 7–8 minutes until cooked to medium-rare. Remove from the oven and rest for 10 minutes before slicing.

Melt the first measure of butter in the same pan you cooked the duck in (with the duck fat removed) over a medium heat. Add the shallot, ginger and five-spice and cook for a few minutes. Turn up the heat and add the red wine. Simmer to reduce by half. Add the chicken stock, sugar, chilli powder, second measure of butter and the berries, then simmer until reduced to the consistency of a thick sauce, 7–10 minutes. Taste and season with salt and pepper.

Pour the sauce over the sliced duck breast and garnish with the spring onion.

Serves 4

Dutch-style slow-cooked beef croquettes

There's a little time involved in making these croquettes, but it's more than worth it. Friends that have dutifully been testing my recipes agreed that this was the 'tastiest little morsel' out of anything I'd given them. The croquettes are easily frozen once you've fried them – then you can just whip them out and reheat in the oven. Serve with relish or tomato sauce.

1kg stewing beef
1 litre water
80g butter
5 tbsp plain flour
½ cup grated tasty cheese
½ cup very finely chopped fresh parsley leaves
salt and freshly cracked black pepper
400g breadcrumbs
3 free-range eggs, lightly beaten
oil for deep-frying

Place the beef and water in a stock pot, cover and simmer for 2½ hours. Remove the meat from the pan and reserve 2½ cups of the cooking liquid – give it a good stir before you set aside the liquid, so you get all the brown stuff from the bottom, too.

Remove the fat and gristle from the meat. Use a fork or your fingers to shred the meat into tiny pieces. I place the meat on a chopping board and just scrape the fork down it so it pulls off easily. Put the meat in a large bowl.

Melt the butter in a saucepan over a medium heat. Add the flour and mix to form a paste. Cook for about 5 minutes but don't let it brown. Slowly pour in the cooking liquid, whisking continuously to avoid lumps forming. Keep cooking and stirring until the sauce thickens, about 5 minutes.

Add the sauce to the beef along with the cheese and parsley, and mix well to combine. Taste and season with salt and pepper. Put the mixture in the fridge for about half an hour to cool.

Place the breadcrumbs in a bowl and the beaten eggs in another. Take about a quarter cup of the beef mixture and roll it into a small sausage shape. Roll in the breadcrumbs to coat lightly. Repeat with the remaining mixture. Dip each croquette in the egg, then roll once more in the breadcrumbs.

Preheat the oven to 50°C.

Heat the oil in a large saucepan over a medium-high heat to about 190°C. Dip in the end of a wooden spoon to test the heat – if bubbles form around it, then the oil is ready. Cook the croquettes in batches until golden brown, turning them over with tongs to cook evenly. Place cooked croquettes on a plate lined with paper towels, and keep warm in the oven. Repeat with the remaining croquettes.

Serves 2

Eye fillet with horseradish butter

Eye fillet is such a lovely creamy cut of steak (not exactly cheap, but for a treat or a special occasion, it's hard to beat). When it's cooked perfectly, it just melts in your mouth. There's no need to smother it in a rich, heavy sauce – this peppery little horseradish butter works just perfectly to bring out the flavour in the meat. An elegant and sophisticated dish that's super easy to make, this is a fabulous way to show off at a dinner party. This recipe can easily be multiplied if feeding a few people.

Butter

50g butter, softened
2–3 tsp horseradish
1 tbsp finely chopped fresh parsley leaves

Eye fillet

400g piece beef eye fillet (square cut)
olive oil
salt and freshly cracked black pepper
1 cup salt-reduced beef stock
1 tbsp cream

Combine the butter, horseradish and parsley, and mix well. Spoon onto a large piece of cling film in a rough log shape. Carefully roll up the cling film by holding each end and rolling up like a Christmas cracker – this will make a nice round log. Place in the freezer.

Preheat the oven to 220°C.

Trim the silver skin carefully off the eye fillet with a sharp knife. Cut into two even-sized pieces. Pat dry with paper towels, then coat with olive oil and season generously all over with salt and pepper.

Heat 1 tablespoon of olive oil in a frying pan over a high heat. Add the eye fillet and sear the sides, about 30 seconds or so each side, until well browned. Place in a roasting tray and roast in the oven for 15 minutes or until cooked to your liking. Remove from the tray, cover with foil and rest for 15 minutes.

While the steak is resting, heat the roasting tray over a medium heat. Add the beef stock to deglaze the tray, scraping up all the stuck-on bits from the bottom. Simmer until the jus has reduced by three-quarters. Add the cream and simmer for a few more minutes. Taste and season with salt and pepper. Strain through a sieve and set aside.

To serve, place the steak on warmed plates. Slice the horseradish butter and place a few slices on the warm steak. Pour the jus over the top. Serve with seasonal vegetables or salad and steamed new potatoes with butter and mint.

Serves 4–6

Eggplant Parmigiana

This dish is based on the Parmigiana I made on *MasterChef*, which Simon Gault called one of the best vegetarian dishes he'd ever tasted. I think even the most staunch meat-eaters would be pleasantly surprised at this dish, because it's very tasty and hugely flavoursome. The goat's cheese and mozzarella add a nice creaminess, and the crumb gives a satisfying crunch which rounds the dish off nicely.

1kg eggplant, cut lengthways into slices 1cm thick
plain flour for dusting
3 tbsp olive oil, plus extra
1 onion, finely chopped
2 cloves garlic, finely chopped
2 tsp tomato paste
¼ cup dry white wine
2 x 400g cans chopped tomatoes
¾ cup freshly grated parmesan
pinch chilli flakes
2 tsp sugar
salt and freshly cracked black pepper
1 cup grated mozzarella (fresh buffalo mozzarella is best, if your budget permits)
50g soft goat's cheese, crumbled
1 cup day-old ciabatta or sourdough, crumbled into course crumbs
extra virgin olive oil to serve

Preheat the oven to 170°C fan-bake.

Dust the eggplant slices in flour. Heat 1 tablespoon of the olive oil in a frying pan over a medium-high heat, then brown the eggplant on each side. You will need to add more oil between batches. Drain on paper towels.

To make the tomato sauce, heat 1 tablespoon of oil in a frying pan over a medium heat. Add the onion, garlic and tomato paste, and cook for 4–5 minutes until the onion is soft. Add the wine, tomatoes, half the parmesan, the chilli flakes and sugar, and simmer gently for 5 minutes. Taste and season with salt and pepper.

Place a layer of eggplant in the bottom of a baking dish. Spread a little of the tomato sauce over, and sprinkle with a little grated mozzarella. Repeat until all the ingredients are used up, reserving a little mozzarella, and finish with a layer of the sauce.

Place the remaining parmesan and mozzarella, the crumbled goat's cheese, breadcrumbs, 1 tablespoon of olive oil and a pinch of salt in a bowl, tossing to combine. Sprinkle over the top of the dish.

Bake in the oven for 30–40 minutes.

Drizzle with a little good-quality extra virgin olive oil and serve with a salad.

Serves 2–3

Seafood fettuccine

I'm a huge sucker for good seafood pasta, to the point where it's very hard for me not to order it if I see it on a menu. This recipe is one of my husband Mike's favourites – it tastes so unbelievably good yet isn't complicated to make. You can add any seafood you like: calamari, clams, mussels, salmon or even crayfish if you are lucky enough to have it! I always keep a bag of prawns in my freezer, so on a busy weeknight sometimes I'll just use lots of those. The only thing to watch out for is overcooking the seafood – it literally only takes a few minutes.

1 tbsp olive oil
1 onion, finely chopped
3 cloves garlic, finely chopped
1 tbsp tomato paste
½ tsp sugar
1 x 400g can chopped tomatoes
375ml fish stock
1 tsp chopped fresh thyme leaves
1 x 400g packet fresh fettuccine
¼ cup cream
zest of 1 lemon
2 tbsp finely chopped fresh parsley leaves
salt and freshly cracked black pepper
1 cup baby spinach leaves
2–3 (approx 500g) fish fillets, chopped into large chunks
1 cup raw prawns, peeled and deveined or 1 cup of seafood of your choice
1 tsp chopped fresh dill
¼ cup freshly grated parmesan
juice of 1 lemon

Heat the oil in a frying pan over a medium heat. Add the onion, garlic, tomato paste and sugar, and sauté for about 5 minutes until the onion is soft. Add the tomatoes, fish stock and thyme leaves, and simmer gently until the liquid is reduced by half – about 15 minutes.

Meanwhile, bring a saucepan of salted water to the boil and cook the pasta according to the packet instructions until al dente. Drain and set aside until needed.

Add the cream, lemon zest and half the parsley to the sauce, and simmer for another few minutes. Taste and season with salt and pepper. Add the spinach, fish and prawns, or seafood of your choice if using, to the sauce. Gently simmer for a few minutes until the fish is only just cooked through. Sprinkle the remaining parsley and the dill and parmesan over the sauce, and add the lemon juice.

Serve over the al dente fettuccine.

Serves 4

Pork with raisins, fennel and pancetta

Pork and fruit go so well together, as odd as it sounds. I created this recipe using raisins as the fruit pairing for something a bit different to the good old pork and apple combo that we all know and love. The little dried grapes work beautifully here, and the crispy pancetta on top takes it to another level. When I was writing this book, I sent this recipe out to a lucky few family members to test – and the feedback was extremely good. It's a winner!

700g pork fillet or rump steaks
1½ tsp fennel seeds, roughly ground in a mortar and pestle
1½ tbsp finely chopped fresh thyme
1 tbsp olive oil
½ tsp salt
½ tsp white pepper
150g pancetta, chopped
25g butter
½ onion, finely diced
3 cloves garlic, finely chopped
½ cup raisins
1 cup chicken stock
¼ cup white wine
¼ cup cream

Preheat the oven to 50°C.

Coat the pork well in the ground fennel seeds, thyme, oil, salt and pepper in a bowl.

Fry the pancetta in a frying pan until crispy. Drain on paper towels and place in the oven to keep warm.

Heat a large non-stick frying pan over a medium-high heat and cook the pork for about 4 minutes on each side until golden brown on the outside and medium-rare in the middle. Remove from the pan, cover and place in the oven to keep warm.

Return the pan to the stove over a medium heat. Add the butter, onion, garlic and raisins, and sauté until soft. Add the chicken stock and wine, then turn up the heat and simmer until reduced by two-thirds. Add the cream and simmer until the sauce is thick enough to coat the back of a spoon.

Remove the pork from the oven and tip the juices into the sauce. Taste and season with salt and pepper.

Serve the pork atop new potatoes and green beans or spinach. Sprinkle the pancetta on top, then pour over the sauce.

Serves 4

My chicken laksa

I've been mildly obsessed with laksa ever since I was lucky enough to cook Rick Stein's recipe for the *MasterChef* final. I never got to keep his recipe but I remember it pretty well, and this is my version of it. The ingredient list might look daunting, but laksa is really not difficult and it tastes so much better when you make your own curry paste. You may have to buy one or two key ingredients you don't already have, but you can use them again and again. And trust me, once you've cooked this dish, you will be asked to make it again! If you want to add prawns as well, they are a welcome addition.

Curry paste

2 tbsp neutral oil (rice bran or canola)
1 shallot, chopped
½ onion, chopped
2 cloves garlic, peeled
2cm piece fresh ginger, peeled and chopped
2 tsp ground cumin seeds
1 tbsp ground coriander seeds
zest of 1 lime
1 tsp ground turmeric
2–3 red chillies, deseeded (more if you like a hot curry!)
1 stalk lemongrass, chopped
1 tbsp shrimp paste (available at Asian supermarkets)

Curry

200g rice vermicelli or stick noodles
oil for cooking
500ml salt-reduced chicken stock
1 x 400ml can coconut cream
4–5 skinless, boneless chicken thighs, chopped into chunks
250g green beans, topped and tailed
1½ tbsp brown or palm sugar
2 tbsp lime juice (use the zested lime from the paste)
2 tbsp fish sauce
¼ cup chopped fresh coriander leaves
your pick of one or all to serve: extra chopped fresh coriander leaves, mung bean sprouts, chopped peanuts and/or chilli

Process all the curry paste ingredients in a food processor or pound in a mortar and pestle to a nice smooth paste.

Soak the noodles in a bowl of boiling water for 8–10 minutes until al dente. Drain and set aside.

Heat a little oil in a wok or saucepan, add the paste and stir-fry over a medium heat for 3–5 minutes. Add the chicken stock and coconut cream, and simmer for about 10 minutes or until the liquid has reduced by a quarter. Add the chicken pieces and simmer until cooked through. Add the beans and cook until just tender. Add the sugar, lime juice and fish sauce. Taste and add more of each until the flavour is balanced to your liking. Stir through the coriander.

Pile the noodles into soup bowls, then ladle the laksa over the top. Garnish with extra coriander, mung bean sprouts, chopped peanuts or extra chilli.

Serves 4

Fish in crazy water (acqua pazza)

This is another of my favourite dishes inspired by summers spent at the beach, catching fresh fish every day and needing many ways to use it up. It's my take on an Italian classic – a fantastic little fish soup/stew dish that delivers amazing flavour. I often serve this when we have guests for dinner, because it's a little bit special and I love the way the tomatoes make the delicately poached fish sing with flavour. Make sure you use the freshest fish possible, as it's the star of the dish. Cooked to perfection, it will melt in your mouth!

Croutons

1 tbsp olive oil
1 tbsp butter
½ day-old ciabatta or sourdough loaf, torn into small pieces
salt

Fish

700g fresh, ripe tomatoes or 2 x 400g cans chopped tomatoes
3 tbsp olive oil
3 large cloves garlic, chopped
1 red chilli, deseeded and finely chopped
½ tsp ground cumin
100ml dry white wine
800ml water
1 tbsp chopped fresh oregano or thyme leaves
2 tsp sugar
1 cup cherry tomatoes, halved
2 tbsp chopped fresh flat-leaf parsley leaves
¼ cup fresh basil leaves, roughly torn
¼ cup chopped fresh coriander leaves
salt and freshly cracked black pepper
700–900g firm white fish fillets
lemon wedges to serve

To make the croutons, heat the olive oil and butter in a frying pan over a medium-high heat. Add the chunks of bread and sauté until the bread is golden and crispy on the outside and soft on the inside. Season with a little salt. Set aside.

If using fresh tomatoes, prepare them by making a cross-shaped cut in the bottom of each tomato, placing in a heatproof bowl and covering with boiling water. Leave for 2 minutes, then remove from the water and peel. Chop the seeds and flesh roughly and discard the hard white core.

Place the olive oil, garlic, chilli and cumin in a large frying pan and cook over a medium heat for a few minutes. Add the tomatoes, wine, water, oregano or thyme leaves and sugar. Cover and simmer gently for 30 minutes. Remove the lid and continue to simmer until the liquid is reduced by half, 20–30 minutes. Stir through the cherry tomatoes, parsley, basil and coriander. Taste and season with salt and pepper.

Lay the fish fillets on top of the sauce and simmer for a minute or so. Very gently turn the fillets over and cook for another minute until the fish is only just cooked through.

Serve in bowls as a stew, sprinkled with the croutons and a squeeze of lemon juice.

Serves 3–4

Lamb rump with anchovies and gremolata

Lamb rump is a regular meal for us because it's so quick and easy to prepare, and rump is jammed with flavour – quite possibly my favourite cut of lamb. Anchovies and lamb are a classic combination – once anchovies are cooked, there is no fishiness there at all, just gorgeous salty flavour. Still, not everyone likes the idea of eating little brined fish, so if you want to hide them, chop them up finely with the gremolata.

2 cloves garlic, very finely chopped
zest of 1 lemon
1 tbsp very finely chopped fresh parsley leaves
1 x 400g lamb rump
salt and freshly cracked black pepper
olive oil for cooking
1 tbsp Dijon mustard
6–7 anchovy fillets

Preheat the oven to 220°C.

Mix the garlic, lemon zest and parsley together.

Season the lamb with a little salt and pepper.

Heat a little olive oil in a frying pan over a high heat. Sear the lamb rump on all sides, for a few minutes total, until browned all over.

Transfer the lamb to a roasting tray. Spread the Dijon mustard over the top, then sprinkle with the zest mixture to evenly coat the top. Lay the anchovy fillets on top and season with another crack of pepper.

Place in the oven for 10–15 minutes until the lamb is medium-rare or cooked to your liking. Rest for 10 minutes before serving.

Serve with seasonal greens or a fresh salad and extra Dijon mustard.

Serves 4–5

Slow-cooked lamb shanks

A tender lamb shank lying provocatively on a bed of creamy mash slathered in a rich, shiny sauce is a sight to warm the very cockles of any heart. The wonderful aromas that fill the house as the lamb slow-cooks drive me crazy! The carrot and the celery are important here for adding flavour to the sauce, but I prefer not to serve them as by the time they finish cooking they're a bit flaccid and drained of all their goodness anyway – so they go in whole and I take them out at the end. This recipe can also be made in a covered slow-cooker set to low when you leave for work in the morning – just add a cup or so more stock. If you can't find lamb stock, half chicken and half beef works too. Serve with creamy mashed potatoes and steamed seasonal veges.

4 large lamb shanks
3 tbsp plain flour
salt and freshly cracked black pepper
3 tbsp olive oil
25g butter
1 onion, finely chopped
1 shallot, chopped
4 cloves garlic, finely chopped
2 tbsp tomato paste
½ bottle red wine
2 tbsp finely chopped fresh thyme leaves
1 cup lamb stock
1 x 400g can chopped tomatoes
1 carrot
1 stick celery
large pinch chilli flakes
1 sprig fresh rosemary
1 bay leaf
1 tsp sugar
chopped fresh parsley leaves to serve
1 tbsp butter

Preheat the oven to 140°C.

Cut through the tendon that connects the meat to the bone at the bottom of each shank. This will allow the meat to bunch up nicely.

Put the flour in a plastic bag with a good amount of salt and pepper. Put the lamb shanks in the bag two at a time and shake to coat.

Heat 2 tablespoons of olive oil in a frying pan, then brown the shanks in batches for a few minutes each side, turning until browned all over. Set the shanks aside.

Add the remaining olive oil, butter, onion, shallot, garlic and tomato paste to the same pan, and cook for 5 minutes over a medium heat until the onion is soft and the tomato paste caramelised. Turn up the heat, add the wine and bring to a rapid simmer. Let it bubble for a minute. Add the thyme, lamb stock and tomatoes. Then add the shanks back to the pan along with the whole carrot, whole celery stick, chilli, rosemary, bay leaf and sugar. If your pan isn't ovenproof or is too small, transfer everything to a large baking dish or casserole.

Cover and cook in the oven for 3½–4 hours, basting and turning the shanks occasionally. Remove from the oven. Gently remove the shanks (they will be delicate) and set aside to rest, covered in foil. Discard the whole carrot and celery.

Place the pan over a medium heat and simmer until reduced to a sauce consistency (you many need to add a little cornflour mixed with water to thicken it up). Add the butter, then taste and season with salt and pepper. To serve, pour the sauce over each shank and sprinkle with parsley.

Serves 4–5

Slow-cooked Moroccan lamb tagine

Lamb necks are an exceptionally tasty cut of meat and far too often overlooked. This flavoursome Moroccan-style recipe is a perfect way to use them. I've only recently purchased a tagine (the baking dish traditionally used to cook the tagine is also called a tagine), and it's wonderful as the convex-shaped lid means the steam runs back down into the dish to retain moisture. If you don't have one, use a covered casserole dish – you'll just need to keep checking the liquid to make sure it doesn't dry up. I would normally pick the meat from the bones before serving, as it's easier for people to eat that way.

2 tsp sweet paprika
1 tbsp ground coriander
1½ tsp ground cumin
½ tsp ground cardamom
½ tsp cayenne pepper
¼ tsp ground cloves
¼ tsp ground turmeric
¼ tsp ground cinnamon
800g lamb necks or shoulder chops (not lean meat)
3 tbsp olive oil
1 onion, finely chopped
2 cloves garlic, finely chopped
1 tsp finely chopped fresh ginger
1 x 400g can chopped tomatoes
1½ cups lamb or chicken stock
1 tbsp honey
zest of 1 lemon
¾ tsp salt
¾ cup prunes or dried apricots
pinch chilli powder (optional)
½ cup plain unsweetened yoghurt to serve
squeeze of lemon

Mix the dry spices together. Brush the lamb with 2 tablespoons of olive oil, then cover in the spice rub. Leave the lamb in the fridge for at least an hour, or overnight would be even better.

Preheat the oven to 140°C.

Heat the remaining oil in a frying pan over a medium-high heat and brown the lamb pieces in batches. Set aside in a tagine or a casserole dish with a lid.

Turn the heat down to medium, add the onion, garlic and ginger to the pan and cook until the onion is soft. Then add the tomatoes, chicken stock, honey, lemon zest and salt. Pour the vegetable mixture over the top of the lamb.

Cook for 2½ hours. Now add the prunes or dried apricots and cook for another half hour. Taste and season with salt and a pinch of chilli if using.

Serve with fluffy couscous and chopped spinach, yoghurt and a squeeze of lemon juice.

Serves 4

Chicken pad Thai

I don't know many people who dislike pad Thai. Making your own is easy and I guarantee it's just as good, if not better than what you'd buy from the local takeaway joint. I got the rough gist of this dish verbally from my husband Mike's best mate, who would always make it for us when we begged. I've worked it into a recipe for you which I can happily say is just as good! If you want to sass it up, add some prawns as well; just pop them in when you add the chicken back to the pan with the capsicum.

1 x 200g packet rice stick noodles
1 tbsp peanut oil
600g boneless, skinless chicken thighs or breasts, chopped into small pieces
1 tsp sesame oil
1 onion, chopped
3 cloves garlic, chopped
1 red capsicum, thinly sliced
2 tbsp brown or palm sugar
2 tbsp fish sauce
2 tbsp lime juice
1–2 red chillies, deseeded and chopped (optional)
2 free-range eggs
½ cup chopped spring onions
1 cup mung bean sprouts
½ cup chopped fresh coriander leaves and stalks
½ cup crushed roasted peanuts
extra chopped chillies and fresh coriander leaves, lime wedges and crushed peanuts to serve

Place the rice stick noodles in a large bowl or saucepan, cover with boiling water, pushing any noodles down that float up as they soften, and leave to soak for 8–10 minutes. Drain, then set aside.

Heat the peanut oil in a large wok or frying pan over a high heat. Add the chicken pieces and stir-fry until golden all over and cooked through. Remove the chicken from the pan and set aside.

Turn the heat down to medium-high and add the sesame oil to the same pan. Then add the onion and garlic and stir-fry for a few minutes until the onion is soft. Add the chicken and red capsicum and stir-fry for another minute. Add the noodles and stir or toss to combine.

Add the brown sugar, fish sauce, lime juice and chillies if using, and stir or toss to combine.

Move everything in the pan to one side and crack in the eggs. Leave for 10–20 seconds then chop the eggs with a spatula, wooden spoon or fish slice, and stir or toss vigorously to incorporate them into the rest of the ingredients.

Add the chopped spring onions and mung bean sprouts and stir. Taste and, if need be, add more sugar, lime juice, fish sauce or chilli to your liking. Stir through three-quarters of the fresh coriander and sprinkle with the crushed peanuts and a little more coriander.

Serve the pad Thai in big bowls. Put the extra chilli, coriander, lime and peanuts in separate little bowls for people to add as they wish.

Serves 4

Pork rice paper rolls

This meal was inspired by a recipe from my friend Ray McVinnie (he really is a food genius). This is my variation of it – it's fresh and light, and the flavours are clean yet robust. A really nice thing about this meal is everyone sitting around the table, chatting away about the day while getting stuck in making their rolls. Yes, bits and pieces go everywhere, water drips all over the table and fingers get rather sticky, but that's half the fun! If you would rather use chicken, it also works well. I've included some ingredients to add to the rolls – use all or some of them or add your own depending on what you have that's in season.

Dipping sauce

2 tbsp fish sauce
1 clove garlic, finely chopped
pinch chilli flakes
1 tbsp brown sugar
1 tbsp lime juice

Pork

800g pork steak, cut into thin strips
2 cloves garlic, finely chopped
1 tbsp ginger juice (finely grate fresh ginger, then squeeze out the juice)
1 tbsp soy sauce
1 tsp sesame oil
peanut or canola oil for frying

To serve

round rice paper wrappers
finely chopped carrot sticks
finely chopped cucumber sticks
finely chopped celery sticks
tomato wedges
roasted peanuts
chopped fresh coriander leaves and stalks
chopped fresh basil leaves
chopped fresh mint leaves

Whisk together all the dipping sauce ingredients in a small bowl until combined and the sugar is dissolved. Taste and, if need be, add more fish sauce, sugar or lime juice until the balance of flavours is to your liking. Set aside.

Combine the pork strips, garlic, ginger juice, soy sauce and sesame oil in a bowl. Cover and pop in the fridge to marinate for 30 minutes, or for longer if you have the time.

Heat the peanut oil in a wok or frying pan over a very high heat. Add the pork in batches and stir-fry until just cooked.

Put the pork, rice paper rounds and a large bowl of lukewarm water on the table along with the dipping sauce and prepared fillings of your choice. Dip a rice paper round in the lukewarm water until softened. Fill with pork and salad ingredients. Roll up, dip into the sauce and enjoy!

Chapter seven

Desserts

Serves 4–6

Apple, rum and raisin tarte Tatin

I just had to include a tarte Tatin recipe in here, because those French were definitely on to something wonderful with this fabulous caramelised upside-down tart. This is my version, and the classic rum and raisin duo goes beautifully with the apple. You do have to watch that the caramel doesn't burn, so I recommend not wandering away from the stove for the first part. If you don't have time to soak the raisins it's not the end of the world, just try it next time. When it's fresh out of the oven, serve it with a lovely scoop of vanilla ice-cream – that's all it needs.

½ cup raisins soaked overnight in 1 cup rum
2 sheets flaky puff pastry
50g butter
100g sugar
1 tbsp lemon juice
zest of 1 lemon
4–5 apples, peeled, cored and cut into quarters
1 tbsp melted butter
vanilla ice-cream to serve

Drain the raisins and reserve a ¼ cup of the rum.

Preheat the oven to 180°C.

Cut a pastry circle to fit the diameter of an ovenproof frying pan. Prick all over with a fork.

Heat the butter, sugar, lemon juice and zest in the ovenproof pan over a medium-high heat, stirring with a wooden spoon to melt the butter. Once the butter is melted, let it bubble away for a few minutes. Add the rum and shake to combine.

Arrange the apples in the pan in a circular pattern, big ends on the outside and rounded side down, leaving a 1cm border between the apple and the edge of the pan – this is so you can tuck the pastry in snugly. Sprinkle the raisins in all the gaps.

Continue to cook for a few more minutes until the sugar and butter starts turning a slightly golden caramel colour (take care not to burn the caramel). As soon as the caramel is golden, place the pastry circle over the top and use a wooden spoon to push the edges down into the caramel. Brush with the melted butter.

Cook in the oven for 25–30 minutes until the pastry is golden brown.

Remove from the oven and, very carefully, using oven mitts and tea towels, tip the tarte out onto a plate. Be careful as the caramel can burn you very badly. Kids, ask an adult to help you with this part. Slice and serve with ice-cream.

Serves 8

Black Doris plum cheesecake

I don't really enjoy the taste of the sickly sweet, processed cheesecakes that you can buy, so I wanted to create a real one with good natural flavours – and this is one of the desserts I'm most proud of. I've always loved tinned Black Doris plums because they just have this incredible texture and sharp sweetness about them that you don't really get with any other tinned fruit. Used in a cheesecake, the plum's tartness is the perfect foil to the creamy filling, and the hint of ginger in the crunchy base adds a touch of spicy warmth. The deep purple hue also looks rather spectacular against the white.

375g gingernut biscuits
100g butter, softened
250g cream cheese
½ cup icing sugar
zest of 1 lemon
2 tbsp lemon juice
1 tsp vanilla essence or paste
1 cup cream, whipped
2 x 850g cans Black Doris plums, drained and pits removed
¼ cup water
3 tsp sugar
3 tsp gelatine

Crumble the biscuits into a coarse crumb either in a food processor or by wrapping the biscuits in a clean tea towel and bashing them with a rolling pin. Mix in the softened butter until well blended.

Press the crumb mixture into the bottom and almost all the way up the sides of a 22cm springform cake tin in an even layer. Cover and place in the fridge for 20 minutes. (You might have some mixture left over, depending on how big your tin is.)

Beat the cream cheese, icing sugar, lemon zest and juice, and vanilla on high speed in an electric mixer or with a hand-held beater until thick and creamy. Fold in the whipped cream. Spread the cream cheese filling evenly over the base, and return the tin to the fridge for another 30 minutes.

Reserve 4 plums and blitz the rest in a blender or food processor until smooth. Set aside.

Heat the water, sugar and gelatine in a small pan, stirring with a fork until the sugar and gelatine are dissolved. Cool slightly, then add to the plum mixture and mix well. Pour on top of the cheesecake. Cut the reserved plums in half and place face down on top and let them sink into the mixture a bit. Cover and refrigerate for at least 2 hours.

Serves 4

Chocolate and raspberry mousse

This lovely chocolate mousse is heavenly without being overly rich, and the raspberries add a nice hint of tart freshness. The end result really relies on the quality of the chocolate; I made the mistake of using cheap cooking melts once when that's all I had, and it didn't taste very good. If you have the inclination or the budget to use Valrhona chocolate, by all means go ahead. If, like me, you're happy with the next best thing, then something like a nice block of 50–60% cocoa chocolate is perfect.

⅓ cup caster sugar
3 free-range eggs, separated
250g good-quality dark chocolate, broken into pieces
¼ cup cream
30g butter, cubed
150ml cream, whipped into soft peaks
1 cup fresh or frozen raspberries
extra raspberries to serve (optional)
cocoa for dusting

Beat the sugar and egg yolks on high speed for around 8 minutes with a hand-held electric beater or an electric mixer until all the sugar has dissolved and the mixture is thick, pale and creamy. You can use a hand beater, but it will take longer – nothing a bit of elbow grease can't take care of!

Beat the egg whites until soft peaks form.

Place the chocolate, the first measure of cream and the butter in a heatproof bowl that fits snugly over a saucepan of gently simmering (not boiling) water, and melt, stirring gently to combine.

Very slowly pour the melted chocolate mixture into the egg yolk mixture with the beater running, and beat until the two mixtures are well combined.

Fold the chocolate mixture into the egg whites until combined. Gently fold in the whipped cream.

Place 5–6 raspberries in the base of each of four ramekins. Pour the mousse mixture on top to fill, and place in the fridge for at least 2 hours to set.

To serve, dust with cocoa and place on small plates with extra fresh raspberries if you like.

Makes about 15

Christmas truffles

It's just not Christmas at Dad and Heather's house without these truffles. Usually we double or triple the recipe, and there still never seems to be enough to cater for my greedy obsession with them! Please don't wait until Christmas to make them, because these bite-sized chocolate delights with chewy raisins are the perfect sweet addition to any cup of tea!

1 cup raisins or sultanas
6 heaped tbsp whole milk powder
2 tbsp cocoa
4 tbsp soft brown sugar
2 tbsp butter
4 tbsp milk
¾ cup desiccated coconut

Place the raisins, milk powder, cocoa and brown sugar in a bowl, and mix well to combine.

Heat the butter and milk until the butter has only just melted. Pour into the bowl with the dry ingredients and combine well. If necessary, refrigerate until firm enough to shape into balls. With clean hands, shape the mixture into walnut-sized balls, then coat them in the coconut.

Store in an airtight container in the fridge for up to a month – if there are any left!

Serves 6

Lemon and lime tartlets

I like lemon tarts to be lovely and tangy, so your mouth *almost* puckers when you taste them . . . but still sweet enough to put a big smile on your dial. I think my little lemon and lime tarts deliver that perfectly. You can make the recipe as one big tart if you prefer, but you may need to adjust the cooking times a little. Just look for golden brown pastry edges; if you undercook the pastry before you put the filling in, it can go soggy later. Everyone's oven is different, so just keep an eye on it.

Pastry
125g unsalted butter
1½ cups plain flour
¼ cup icing sugar
2 free-range egg yolks

Filling
6 free-range eggs
¾ cup caster sugar
pinch salt
1 cup cream
zest and juice of 2 limes
¾ cup lemon juice
Greek yoghurt or whipped cream to serve
icing sugar to serve
fresh berries to serve

Preheat the oven to 170°C (don't use fan-bake).

To make the pastry, place the butter, flour and icing sugar in a food processor and process until the mixture forms coarse crumbs. With the motor running, add the egg yolks and process until a ball of dough forms. You may need to add a little cold water if the ball does not form on its own. Flatten the pastry into a disc shape and wrap in cling film. Rest in the fridge for 30 minutes.

Remove the dough from the fridge and divide it in half. Roll out each half on a lightly floured bench to a 4mm thickness. Set out 6 x 8cm tart cases. Place the pastry over one of the tart cases and gently coax it into the corners while ensuring the pastry still reaches the top edge of the case. Be careful not to tear it. Gently press the pastry into the grooves in the sides of the tin and so it sits flush with the top edge. Roll the pin over the edge of the case to trim off the excess pastry. Prick the pastry with a fork and repeat with the remaining cases and pastry. Return to the fridge for 15 minutes.

Place the tart cases on a baking tray. Bake in the oven for 15–17 minutes or until the sides are golden. If undercooked at this point, the cases will go soggy later. Remove from the oven but keep them on the oven tray.

To make the filling, gently whisk the eggs, sugar, salt, cream, lime zest and juice, and lemon juice together until the sugar has dissolved and the egg is well incorporated. Pour the filling into each tart case almost to the top. Very carefully return to the oven and bake for another 13–15 minutes or until the filling is still slightly wobbly in the middle.

Cool, then remove from the tart tins and serve with Greek yoghurt or cream, a dusting of icing sugar and fresh berries.

Makes about 20

Olie bollen

Olie bollen is a traditional Dutch dessert. I guess you could liken them to Dutch doughnuts, as they are cooked in a similar way. Mum's Dutch cousins made them for us when they came to stay one New Year's. It was the first time we had tried them and we were all blown away. Crispy, sweet, soft, sugary, amazing! You'll probably need to do a few test ones at the start to get the cooking time right – break them open to check the middle is fluffy and not gooey.

1 cup raisins
½ cup currants
1 cup sweet dessert wine (optional)
1 Granny Smith apple, peeled, cored and finely chopped
zest and juice of 1 lemon
500ml milk
2 tsp caster sugar
2½ tsp dried yeast
500g plain flour
1 tsp salt
1 free-range egg, lightly beaten
rice bran or canola oil for frying
icing sugar to serve

If you like, you can soak the raisins and currants in the dessert wine overnight. If not, just omit the dessert wine and use the fruit as is.

Combine the chopped apple and lemon zest and juice in a small bowl, and set aside.

Gently heat the milk to warm it up (around 40°C – be careful not to overheat it or it will kill the yeast). Transfer ½ a cup or so of the milk into a small bowl, then whisk in the sugar. Sprinkle in the yeast and whisk well to combine. Stand for about 10 minutes until the yeast has frothed up.

Sift the flour and salt into a large bowl (preferably metal or plastic, not ceramic). Make a well in the centre and pour in the yeast mixture and the rest of the warm milk and the egg. Mix to form a smooth batter. Add the apple, raisins and currants (drained of the wine) and mix gently to combine. Cover with a clean damp tea towel or cling film and rest in a warm place (such as the hot water cupboard or above a warm oven) until double in size; this may take up to 1 hour.

Heat the oil in a large saucepan to around 180°C. Dip in the end of a wooden spoon to test the heat – if bubbles form around it, then the oil is ready.

Shape the dough into balls using two oiled dessertspoons. Fry the olie bollen in batches, a few at a time, in the hot oil until they are golden brown. Remove and drain on paper towels. Do not fry too many at the same time, as the temperature of the oil should remain constant. Dust generously with icing sugar and serve immediately.

Allow leftover olie bollen to cool, then store them in an airtight container at room temperature for up to two days. Leftovers can be warmed in a 200°C oven for about 15 minutes.

Serves 4–5

Sticky date puddings

This heavenly dessert doesn't really need much of an introduction. It's sweet, sticky and decadent – just look at it, sitting there on the plate swamped with warm caramel sauce and melty ice-cream. What a perfect way to finish a dinner party and leave your guests in a pleasant state of sweet euphoria! Better yet, they are quick and easy to prepare.

Puddings

1 cup water
400g dates, pitted and roughly chopped
125g butter
1 tbsp golden syrup
¼ cup sugar
1 tsp baking soda
2 free-range eggs, lightly beaten
1 cup plain flour
zest of 1 lemon
2 tsp ground cinnamon

Sauce

50g butter
½ cup soft brown sugar
1 cup cream
1 tsp vanilla essence

vanilla ice-cream to serve

Preheat the oven to 160°C. Grease 4–6 ramekins.

Put the water, dates, butter, golden syrup and sugar in a saucepan and boil for 3 minutes. Remove from the heat.

Add the baking soda and whisk well to combine. Add the eggs, flour, lemon zest and cinnamon, and mix to combine. Pour into the prepared ramekins and bake for about 40 minutes.

To make the sauce, heat all the ingredients in a saucepan over a medium heat until the sugar has dissolved. Bring to the boil, then reduce the heat and simmer for 5 minutes or until the sauce becomes a lovely golden caramel colour. Pour over the puddings and serve with vanilla ice-cream.

Serves 3

Strawberries and cream mille feuille

This is a simple, fresh summery dessert that looks great and requires very few ingredients. The only thing that needs a little TLC is the pastry, which is fried with icing sugar – a fabulous technique I was taught by my pal Dave. In the absence of strawberries, try it with any other berries or tangy fruit such as mango. The crispy, sugary pastry with the juicy strawberries and velvety creamy blobs is a heavenly combination.

½ cup icing sugar
1 tbsp ground cinnamon
1 tbsp ground nutmeg
1 sheet flaky puff pastry
1 punnet juicy ripe strawberries, hulled and quartered
¾ cup thick sweetened Greek yoghurt
1 cup cream, whipped
icing sugar for dusting

Mix the icing sugar, cinnamon and nutmeg together in a bowl. Sprinkle a generous amount on a clean benchtop. Place the sheet of pastry on top, then dust another layer of the icing sugar mix on top. Roll the pastry outwards from the top and bottom to elongate it into a long thin rectangle, so it's a third of its original thickness – it won't cook through if it's any thicker. Cut the rectangle lengthwise into three even-sized strips, then crosswise into three even-sized portions so you have nine even-sized rectangles. Dust with a little more icing sugar mixture on each side.

Heat a large frying pan over a low heat, and place in as many pasty pieces as will fit comfortably. Cook them for a couple of minutes, then turn over. Continue to cook for about 7–10 minutes, turning each piece frequently so the pastry becomes golden brown all over and cooked through. It will burn if left too long on one side, so don't wander off for this part. Place the pastry on a wire rack to cool and repeat with the remaining pieces.

To assemble, place some strawberry pieces on a cooled pastry rectangle. Spoon some Greek yoghurt and whipped cream in the gaps. Gently press another pastry rectangle on top and repeat the process. Top with a third piece of pastry, and dust the top with icing sugar.

Chapter eight

Basics

Mayonnaise

Makes about 1 cup

1 free-range egg
2 tsp Dijon mustard
1 tsp lemon juice
1 cup neutral oil (rice bran or canola)
salt

Blitz the egg, mustard and lemon juice in a food processor or whisk together by hand until well combined. Add the oil in a very thin stream, continuing to process or whisk the whole time. When all the oil is incorporated and the mayonnaise has thickened, taste and season with salt.

Store in an airtight container in the fridge for up to a week.

Aïoli

Makes about 1 cup

1 free-range egg
1 large clove garlic, finely chopped
1 tsp lemon juice
1 cup neutral oil (rice bran or canola)
2 tsp wholegrain mustard
sea salt

In a small food processor, blitz the egg, garlic and lemon juice until pale and well combined. With the motor running, slowly add the oil in a very thin stream until it's all used up – this might take a few minutes. The mixture will slowly thicken.

Add the mustard and blend to combine. Check the seasoning, then add salt until it tastes to your liking.

Store in an airtight container in the fridge for up to a week.

Pesto

Makes about ½ cup

¼ cup pinenuts
1 cup lightly packed fresh basil leaves
⅓ cup parmesan
1 clove garlic
4 tbsp extra-virgin olive oil
2 tsp lemon juice
salt and freshly cracked black pepper

Lightly toast the pinenuts in a dry frying pan over a medium heat for a couple of minutes until only lightly coloured. Put all the ingredients, except the salt and pepper, in a food processor and blitz until still slightly chunky (not super smooth). Taste and add salt until it's salty enough for your liking. Season with pepper.

You can easily double this recipe if you need more. Store in the fridge in an airtight container for a week.

Tartare sauce

Makes about 1½ cups

1 cup mayonnaise (see opposite)
½ cup finely chopped gherkin
2 tsp chopped capers
1 tsp finely chopped fresh parsley leaves
1 tsp finely chopped dill
1 tsp Dijon mustard
2 tsp very finely chopped shallot
1 spring onion, very finely chopped
3 tsp lemon juice
¼ tsp cayenne pepper
salt and freshly cracked black pepper

Mix all the ingredients together. Taste and add more salt, pepper or lemon juice until the flavours are to your liking.

Store in the fridge in an airtight container or jar for up to 2 weeks.

Vinaigrette

Makes ½ cup

3 tbsp extra virgin olive oil
1 tbsp white wine vinegar
1 tsp Dijon mustard
1 tsp finely chopped fresh thyme leaves (or herbs of your choice)
½ tsp sugar

Whisk all the ingredients together in a bowl or process in a food processor until well combined.

Store in the fridge in an airtight jar or bottle for about a month.

Guacamole

Makes about 1 cup

3 large ripe avocados
1 clove garlic, finely chopped
1 tbsp lemon juice
salt and freshly cracked black pepper
pinch chilli flakes (optional)

Scoop out the avocado flesh with a spoon. Place the flesh in a bowl with the garlic and lemon juice, and mash well with a fork until smooth. Season with salt and lots of pepper. Add more lemon juice if you like and a pinch of chilli flakes.

Hummus

Makes about 1½ cups

This hummus recipe is by none other than my big brother Simon. Many years ago (back when hummus definitely wasn't as well known as it is now), he wrote up the recipe in our Great Barrier bach cookbook, and described it as 'A fancy dip to eat with a cold beer on a hot day'. I'm not sure about the 'fancy' part, but he definitely got the rest of it right!

½ batch:

- 1 — *1 whole head garlic*
- 1 - not quite drained — *2 x 425g cans chickpeas, drained*
- 2 — *3 tbsp lemon juice*
- 1 — *2 tsp toasted cumin seeds*
- 2 — *3 tbsp extra virgin olive oil*
- 1 — *2 tbsp tahini*
- *¼ tsp white pepper*
- *salt*

Preheat the oven to 160°C.

Cut the end off the bulb of garlic so the cloves are exposed. Wrap in foil and bake for 1 hour. Cool, then squeeze the roasted garlic out of its skins.

Place all the ingredients in a food processor and process to the desired consistency. Taste and season with salt until salty enough for your liking. At this point you can add more lemon juice, pepper or tahini to balance the flavours.

Serve with crispy pita bread and vegetable sticks, or spread on sandwiches.

Store in an airtight container in the fridge for a week.

Babaganoush

Makes about 1 cup

- *700g (2 medium) eggplants*
- *¼ cup tahini*
- *¼ cup lemon juice*
- *1 clove garlic, chopped*
- *1 tbsp extra virgin olive oil*
- *salt and freshly cracked black pepper*

Preheat the grill to 200°C.

Prick the eggplants all over with a fork about 15 times. Place on a baking tray under the grill for 15 minutes, turning over every few minutes until evenly cooked.

Reduce the oven temperature to 160°C and change the setting to bake. Cook the eggplant for another 10 minutes. Remove from the oven and cool slightly.

Top the eggplants, cut in half and scoop out the flesh and seeds. Place the flesh and seeds in a food processor with the tahini, lemon juice and garlic. Pulse for a few seconds to combine, scraping the sides once with a spatula to incorporate everything. (Don't go crazy with the processing; it doesn't have to have a superfine texture.) Slowly pour in the olive oil and process to just mix through. Wait until the mixture is cool, then taste and season with salt and pepper. If need be, add more lemon juice or tahini until the flavours are balanced to your liking.

Serve with crusty pita bread pieces or on sandwiches or wraps.

Store in the fridge in an airtight container for up to a week.

Tomato relish

Makes about 2 cups

1.5kg fresh ripe tomatoes, cored and roughly chopped
400g red onion, chopped
300g white onion, chopped
¾ cup brown sugar
100ml malt vinegar
100ml white wine vinegar
2 tsp salt
1 tbsp mustard powder
¼ tsp cayenne pepper

Place the tomatoes, both types of onion, sugar and both vinegars in a large saucepan over a high heat and mix together well. Bring to the boil, then turn down to a simmer. Add the salt, mustard powder and cayenne pepper. Simmer until the mixture is reduced to a thick sauce consistency, 1–2 hours. Bottle in sterilised preserving jars (see below).

To sterilise jars, preheat the oven to 160°C. Wash the jars and lids with hot soapy water, then rinse well.

Arrange the jars and lids open side up, without touching, on a tray. Place in the oven for 25 minutes. Or boil the jars and lids for 15 minutes in a large saucepan filled with enough water to cover them.

Sterilise tongs by dipping in boiling water for a few minutes, then use to move the jars from the boiling water or oven.

Carefully pour in your preserves, screw on the lids and leave to cool. Only hot preserves go into hot jars – if you put cold preserves in, you risk cracking the glass.

Tomato sauce

Makes about 3 cups

¼ cup olive oil
1 red onion, chopped
1 white onion, chopped
4 cloves garlic, chopped
1 apple or 1 peach, cored or pitted and chopped
1 carrot, chopped
1 celery stick, chopped
1 red capsicum, deseeded and chopped
½ fennel bulb, chopped
2kg fresh ripe tomatoes, cored and chopped
½ tsp allspice
½ tsp ground ginger
½ tsp chilli powder
600ml water
¾ cup brown sugar
¾ cup wine vinegar
salt and freshly cracked black pepper

Heat the olive oil in a large stock pot over a medium heat. Add both types of onion, the garlic, apple or peach, carrot, celery, capsicum and fennel. Cook, stirring, until the vegetables are soft, 8–10 minutes. Add the tomatoes, allspice, ginger, chilli and water, and stir to combine. Simmer gently, uncovered, until the mixture has reduced by half, stirring every now and then. Process the sauce in a food processor or blender or with a stick blender until very smooth. Pass through a sieve twice. Place the sauce back into the rinsed-out stock pot and add the brown sugar and vinegar. Bring to a simmer and continue to simmer for 15–20 minutes or until the mixture is a nice sauce consistency. Taste and season with salt and pepper.

Pour into hot sterilised bottles or jars while still hot, and seal.

Chargrilled capsicums

Preheat your grill to high.

Place as many capsicums as you need under the grill and cook until the skin is charred and blackened, turning them every now and then to cook evenly. Remove from the oven and place in a plastic bag. Seal the top, then leave for 15–20 minutes. Peel the skins off the capsicums, with the help of a paring knife if you need to. Cut in half and discard the tops, seeds and white membranes. Drizzle with olive oil and keep in an airtight container in the fridge for up to 2 weeks.

Stuffing for roast chicken

½ loaf day-old sourdough or ciabatta, crumbled into small pieces
½ cup plain unsweetened yoghurt
1 tbsp finely chopped rosemary leaves
½ cup chopped bacon
zest of 1 lemon
½ red onion, finely chopped
2 cloves garlic, very finely chopped
½ tsp salt
freshly cracked black pepper

Mix all the ingredients together and stuff the bird.

Lemon curd

Makes about 1½ cups

2 free-range egg yolks
1 whole free-range egg
2 tbsp lemon zest
½ cup lemon juice
¾ cup sugar
50g butter, cubed

Beat the egg yolks, whole egg, lemon zest and juice, and sugar together until well combined. Place in a heatproof bowl that fits snugly over a saucepan of gently simmering water (ensure the bowl is not touching the water).

Stir the mixture continuously while it heats for 8–10 minutes. The mixture will start to thicken as the egg cooks. Be careful not to overcook the eggs or they will scramble – they should be no hotter than 71°C if you have a thermometer.

Add the butter a cube at a time and whisk in, incorporating each cube before adding the next.

Strain the mixture through a sieve, pour into a nice sterilised jar and seal. Keeps in the fridge for a week.

Naan bread

Makes 8 naan

Naan bread has a very special texture and taste – I think it's the perfect accompaniment to any type of curry, even non-Indian ones. I've always bought the frozen kind, but lately I've started making my own and the difference is so remarkable that I find it hard to eat anything else. Just go with whatever toppings you feel like at the time, or have them plain, salted and buttered. You can freeze some of the dough once you've made it into balls so you can quickly whip up the naan at any time.

2 cups plain flour
¼ tsp salt
¾ tsp baking powder
½ tsp baking soda
½ tbsp sugar
½ cup warm milk
½ cup plain unsweetened yoghurt
½ tbsp oil
topping of your choice: cumin seeds, minced garlic, herbs or brush with butter or extra virgin olive oil
salt

Place all the dry ingredients in a large bowl and mix together well. Make a well in the centre.

Mix the warm milk, yoghurt and oil together, then add three-quarters into the well in the flour. Mix gently, and keep adding more of the liquid while mixing until a nice soft dough ball forms. Cover the bowl and leave in a warm place (such as the hot water cupboard) for 2 hours to rise.

Remove the dough from the bowl and knead it gently on a floured surface for a few minutes. Divide the dough into about eight pieces.

Dust a chopping board with flour and flatten and stretch out a piece of dough until it's roughly a naan shape and size. Set aside on a floured bench and repeat with the other pieces. Now sprinkle cumin seeds, minced garlic, herbs or butter on the top of each naan. Sprinkle with a little salt.

Heat a heavy-based frying pan over a high heat. Pick up a naan, brush the underside with water and then place wet side down in the pan. Cook for about 30 seconds or until bubbles start to appear in the bread. If you have a gas stovetop, pick up the naan with tongs and cook the other side directly over the flame for a lovely charred effect. Otherwise, just turn the naan over and cook another minute or so in the pan. Repeat with remaining naan.

Spread with a bit more butter or olive oil and enjoy!

Acknowledgements

As a humble first-time author, I certainly couldn't have produced a book like this without the help of many wonderful people. I'd like to say a thousand thank yous, many times over, to:

Kieran Scott and **Tam West**, for the 'mean-as' photography and styling for the book. It was a privilege to work with two very cool people with such extraordinary talent.

Ray McVinnie, for always making the time to patiently help me solve whatever food dilemma I've got myself in, and for your unbiased advice and guidance.

Tim and Simon at Neat Meat, for generously supplying all the meat (all of it free-range and cruelty-free) for this book. The best quality meat I've ever cooked with or eaten.

Cindi, Darryl and the *MasterChef* crew for making this whole experience possible – *MasterChef* has completely changed my life.

Everyone who tested and critiqued my recipes as I was developing them (especially Dave McGibbon). Hopefully most of the time it was a pleasant experience!

Jenny and the fantastic team at Random House, whose hard work and efficiency have made the (somewhat daunting) task of creating a cookbook a seamless and snag-free one for me. Not to mention enjoyable!

Heather (aka Hot Hev), for your tireless recipe testing and kitchen assistance – you probably never want to see a carrot cake again.

My amazing family and friends, for always being there for me, no matter what.

My husband Mike – a good man with the best heart – for keeping me grounded and always being a (rather handsome) pillar of support.

To everyone else I haven't mentioned who has helped me along the way – you know who you are, thank you.

Finally, this book is dedicated to my mum, Annemieke Farmilo. Thank you for 28 years of unwavering positivity, energy and unconditional love. Without the happiness and self-belief you've instilled in me, this book wouldn't be in existence. You are amazing, and everything I'd like to be.

W

Index

D

E

F

G

T

V